No Greater Love

the
Helen Baylor
Story

Vision
PUBLISHING
Carson, California

Unless otherwise indicated, all Scripture references are taken from the King James Version of the Bible.

No Greater Love
The Helen Baylor Story
ISBN: 0-9762730-0-4
Copyright 2007 by:
James and Helen Baylor

Library of Congress Cataloging-in-Publication Data

Baylor, Helen.
  No greater love : my story / by Helen Baylor.
      p. cm.
  Includes bibliographical references and index.
  ISBN-13: 978-0-9762730-0-4 (pbk. : alk. paper)
  ISBN-10: 0-9762730-0-4 (alk. paper)
  1. Baylor, Helen. 2. African American gospel singers—Biography. 3. Gospel singers—United States—Biography. I. Title.
    ML420.B138A3 2006
    782.25'4092—dc22

                                    2006005144

Published by:
Vision Publishing
P.O. Box 11166
Carson, California 90746-1166
1-800-478-7925

DEDICATION

This book is dedicated to the memory of both my grand-mothers—Mrs. Minnie Hudson (1903-2004) and Mrs. Frances Lowe (1914-2005).

TABLE OF CONTENTS

ACKNOWLEDGMENTS

I would like to express my deepest gratitude and appreciation to the people who have impacted my life most—first, my husband, James, and our children, Jeffrey, Jovan, James II, and Jonathan. You guys are the greatest. I love you.

To Pastor Dale C. and First Lady Nina Bronner. We are so proud to be members of Word of Faith Family Worship Cathedral. Thank you for loving and receiving us.

To my father in the faith, Dr. Frederick K.C. Price, and his lovely wife, Dr. Betty, for teaching me the uncompromised Word of God when I first received Jesus, and for being godly examples for me and my family. Drs. Fred and Betty, you are true jewels.

To my parents, Mr. and Mrs. E.C. Lowe, for being there for me and encouraging me to follow my dreams. To Kenneth A. Lowe, my brother and friend, for the unwavering love and support you've shown me my whole life.

To my friends, Dimawi Denmon, Yvonne and Bill Maxwell, Johnnie and Don Payne, Tony Maiden, Jay and Doris Newsome, and the many others who have been there for me and my family through thick and thin.

To Stanley and Corliss Williford, for your encouragement and hard work in making this dream come true.

And most of all, to my Lord and Savior Jesus Christ, without whose love there would not be a victorious ending to my life story. Thanks for giving your life for mine... there truly is No Greater Love.

INTRODUCTION

Writing this book has been one of the hardest things I've ever done. When you share your testimony, you have to dig up things that have been buried deep in your subconscious memory for a long, long time. You have to talk about people, places and events that are often very painful to recall. At the same time, you must be considerate of other people's feelings and careful not to violate anyone's privacy.

Sitting down and writing this book has been a very tedious thing for me to do. I've been most concerned about how my children would feel knowing so many intimate details of my life. I've talked with them and they have all said in one way or another, "Mommy, go for it! You're gonna help someone." God has assured me that many lives will be touched, that people can take this book to places where a tape, CD, or DVD could not go. People can read this book and pass it on to others.

God has witnessed to me that He is going to win many, many souls because of my obedience in writing my life's story. Of course, the story of my life is like a lot of other life stories. The biggest difference and the best part of *The Helen Baylor Story* is the ending.

Actually, the end of the story marks a brand-new beginning for me. I got saved, I got delivered from drugs and many other carnal things, and you would think,

"Okay, that's the end of the book." No, it most certainly is not! It's only the beginning of my life.

If there is anything, any major thing, I would like readers to take from reading *No Greater Love: The Helen Baylor Story*, it is that, after I came to the Lord and was delivered and set free, I had to start life all over again. From that point on, I have based everything I do on obedience to God's Word—from getting married, to turning my back on secular music, to ultimately preaching the gospel.

When I "sat down" for six years at Crenshaw Christian Center (CCC), my home church at the time, and remained silent as a featured singer, it was out of obedience to God and His Word. I applied myself to learning, went to Bible study weekly, and attended Sunday services. I became involved in the ministry of helps at CCC, doing whatever I could to help my pastor, Dr. Frederick K.C. Price.

I also worked for the church, doing the best job I could as an employee. All these things I did in obedience to God's Word. So it was not my talent, my God-given gift to sing, that opened doors for me, as much as it was my obedience. The Word of God says that our gifts will make room for us and bring us before great men (Proverbs 18:16). But I believe obedience made a way for my gift to open the doors.

As I was obedient to God's Word, doors began to open for me musically. I began to sing in the choir, I began to minister in music for the women's fellowship. I ministered in song wherever the doors opened. God began to supernaturally bring in finances so I could record a four-song cassette. I was then given an opportunity to sign with Word Records. Finally, when I was in the right place, and in His timing, God began to use me to share the gospel and give my testimony of salvation and deliverance through faith in Jesus Christ.

Out of obedience to God's Word, I had to learn to die to self and share with people what the Lord had brought me out of. God began to use me to counsel others, to minister to people over the telephone, to sing and testify, and even to lay hands on the sick.

Sometimes during those six years of preparation, my family and I would not even know where the rent was coming from. I knew it would be on time because I walked "by faith and not by sight" (2 Corinthians 5:7).

Because God had never let us down, and because we knew Him as a supernatural God, we put one foot in front of the other and walked the path He set before us. I would go where He sent me and pour out my heart to the people of God and sinners alike. God would then supernaturally bless us abundantly "above all that we could ask or think" (Ephesians 3:20). I give God alone the glory and the praise. I have always been a tither and a giver, and God has been faithful to open the windows of heaven for me and my family (Malachi 3:10).

So now wherever I go, in obedience to God's Word and in obedience to what He is telling me by His Spirit, my emphasis is, and always will be, on souls. My emphasis is not on selling CDs. My emphasis is not on filling up auditoriums or winning awards. I go to churches where my primary goal is to share the Good News of Jesus Christ and to see lives changed. I never major on ticket sales or big productions. I will go wherever God sends me. As I am obedient, God continues to be faithful.

After I have prayerfully considered every invitation to sing or to speak, I can still only accept perhaps a third of those I receive. At least two-thirds involve scheduling conflicts, or are outside of God's perfect timing for me.

I am scheduled a year in advance. My husband, James, and I do not make up our schedule according to managerial advice or with the help of agents. It is all happening by God's grace in accordance with His divine purpose for our lives.

And, as we have been obedient to what God has called us to do, God has opened the doors. However, some have said to me from time to time that I really do not have to share my testimony about drugs and alcohol or the lifestyle I led before I came to the Lord.

Some tell me that I should not speak openly about the low self-esteem, which I dealt with for years, even after becoming a Christian. They say that people love me for my music. I believe that even though my music would be enough, I am compelled to share all of me to truly give God the glory He is due. It is not very comfortable for me to share some things. Nevertheless, in spite of my discomfort, for the last sixteen years or so I have been given prophecies regarding my writing a book based on my testimony. These prophecies were always comforting to me because they confirmed what was already in my heart.

My story was not over when I received Jesus Christ as Lord and Savior. The story of my new life had just begun. My testimony of what happened in my old life, however, makes it very clear that God's awesome power to save, heal and deliver is real. I am no longer a pawn to be used and ultimately destroyed by Satan, but I have become a trophy of God's magnificent grace.

My prayer is that this book will touch the life of every reader, that those who are without hope will find hope in Jesus Christ, and those who are praying for unsaved loved ones will be encouraged to fight the good fight of faith. Jesus Christ is no respecter of persons. What He did for me, He will do for anyone who asks.

HELEN BAYLOR
April, 2007

1

In the Beginning

Not long before I was born, my parents, Melva Kelly Lowe and Ennis Lowe, who were seventeen and eighteen years old at the time, moved from Tulsa, Oklahoma, to Oceanside, California.

My dad was born in Holdenville, Oklahoma. He was raised in Wetumka, Oklahoma, along with two sisters and four brothers, until he was about twelve or thirteen. Then his family moved to Tulsa, where he lived until he joined the Marine Corps.

My mom was born in Henderson, Texas, and was raised in Tulsa after living in St. Louis, Missouri, for a couple of years as a very young girl. When it was discovered that my mom was pregnant, she and my dad married in a civil ceremony on September 27, 1952. Later, Dad joined the U.S. Marine Corps and subsequently was stationed at Camp Pendleton in Oceanside.

My dad left for California a couple of months before my mom joined him in the fall of 1952, and they were together just a few months before I was born in January, 1953. Four years later, by the time my mother and father were twenty and twenty-one, they had four children, who were like little stair steps. My only sister, Diane, was born thirteen months behind me, and then two brothers—Ennis,

Jr., and Kenneth—were also born thirteen months apart. Over the next thirteen years, four more sons were born to the Lowe family—Gary, Jeffrey (who passed away shortly after birth), Marlon, and Jason.

After Dad's term of service was over, my parents took Ennis, Jr., and me back to Tulsa. Diane remained with my mother's aunt, Dezelle, and Uncle John in Long Beach, California.

Shortly after our return to Oklahoma—when I was about three or four years old—I was sent to live with my paternal grandparents. I called my grandfather "Daddy Bo," and I called my grandmother "Mama Frances." Their youngest children, my aunt and two of my uncles, were still living at home, so I became the immediate "baby" in the family. It felt as though my uncles and aunt were my older brothers and sister. I was babied some days and teased on others, and I soon turned into the typical brat who got practically everything she wanted, although there wasn't a lot to want back then. I was a spoiled, whiny, and sometimes bossy child.

My grandparents' home seemed huge to me as a little girl. It was a beautiful white house out in the country with hardwood floors and comfortable furnishings. But, I must tell you, it was a real "country" house with few of the amenities we take for granted today.

There was a huge garden at the side of the house adjacent to the dirt road. I can still remember my grandfather quartering "seed" potatoes and putting them into the ground. At five and six years old, I marveled at the fact that, after a while, we could go to the garden and dig up whole potatoes. Daddy Bo grew corn and tomatoes and other vegetables. He had pigs and hunting dogs, too, some of the laziest, homeliest-looking dogs you ever wanted to see. It was a great place to grow up, but years later, when I went back to visit, the place looked small and dinky, nothing like what I remembered. I suppose this is typical of most childhood homes. Things look so much larger to children.

As I think of that old house, I realize how much I enjoyed living there as a child. We especially had good Christmases. My dad's youngest sister, Clara, who was still living at home, used to do my hair. She would press it, using our old stove to heat the hot comb and curling iron. In fact, almost everything we did was done around that stove.

We cooked, heated water to wash dishes, and heated water for baths and water to wash clothes on that stove. Our clothes were washed in an old rotary-type wringer washing machine. After the clothes were rinsed, they were run through the two-cylinder wringer, which pressure-squeezed as much water out as possible. Our clothes were then hung on a clothesline in the yard to dry in the sun.

We heated water for our baths on Friday or Saturday. A large galvanized tub was placed in the middle of the kitchen floor. We would draw enough water from the well outside to heat and pour it into the tub. Then we would take our baths and keep adding hot water to keep it warm.

The last person to take a bath didn't have it so good. In fact, even to me as a little kid, the water was kind of gross by that time. I was always happy when I got to take my bath first.

There was an outhouse (an outdoor toilet) because the plumbing in the bathroom didn't work since there was no running water in the house. I hated the outhouse because it was so smelly, and it was a good distance from the house. There was something called a chamber pot that sat in the bathroom. Anyone who had to use the bathroom in the middle of the night would use this pot. Then one of the older kids had to empty it in the morning.

That was the only kind of home I knew, and I thought everyone lived like that. I did not know, until I moved back with my mom and dad when I was about seven years old, that bathrooms were supposed to work. Growing up there was good for me in a lot of ways. I wouldn't trade those early years for anything.

Our floors were made of beautiful hardwood, except for the kitchen and bathroom. My grandfather worked for a large janitorial company and he would bring home his buffer sometimes to do our floors. It looked like so much fun when he used it. Sometimes he'd let me ride on it while he buffed the floors. He would slowly move it back and forth, and I would hold on and giggle. The floors got a good buffing, and I got a fun ride out of the deal. One day, I turned it on with no pads or brushes underneath, and that buffer jerked me around like a little rag doll and ground up the dining room floor, leaving huge scratches and a shallow hole in it.

I was surprised when I did not get a spanking for my misbehavior that day. I got yelled at, though, which to me was worse. I can remember my uncles laughing at me. "You gon' git in trouble," they would say. My grandfather was so disappointed in me, which made me feel terrible for a long time after that. I do remember that he replaced the wooden planks, and as far as I could see, made the floor as good as new.

Also, there was a huge, old piano in the dining room, which figures into some of my earliest memories of music. My Aunt Clara would sit on the piano bench, and I would crawl up next to her and watch her play. I knew then that I really loved music. She played only simple songs and the boogie-woogie. She would teach me how to do the right hand and then the left hand. Then we would play together.

Clara collected every new song that came out on 45-rpm records and played them in the evenings after she got home from school. Hearing them over and over, I soon learned the words to the songs. I also learned the different dances that were popular then: the jitterbug and other dance steps the older kids were doing.

I tried to do everything they did. I would sing along with the records and dance in some of Clara's old clothes. Sometimes she would put a little makeup on me, and I would sing. And I knew in my heart right then what I wanted to do. I wanted to entertain people. It seems the Lord put a desire for music in my heart early in life, but immediately, the enemy came to try to pervert that desire and even destroy my life.

I remember watching Ed Sullivan on my grand-mother's black and white console television. We really liked "The Ed Sullivan Show," so every Sunday night we gathered around the television as a family. I loved the drama, excitement, and glamour of show business. There was no question in my mind that if I ever got a chance to live out my heart's desire, I would someday be involved in show business.

Life with my grandparents began to be unstable after a while. My grandfather and grandmother were having marital problems, so he started staying away at nights. I can remember my grandfather being there in the evening, but not in the morning. I asked him once, "Daddy Bo, why aren't you here when I wake up in the morning? Where have you been? Have you been working? What are you doing? Why don't you sleep here at night anymore?" He gave me some kind of answer that put me off, but things felt uneasy from then on. We found out later that he had a girlfriend on the side. When I look back on the whole situation, it was confusing to me as a child. However, my grandparents seemed to have an understanding between them.

I know Mama Frances didn't like what was going on, but they seemed to have worked things out somehow. I never heard them arguing or fighting over it. He never stopped taking care of Mama Frances and the rest of us. I don't know what precipitated the change in our family life, but all of a sudden there was this breach between them. Then other things began to change a little bit, as well. We kids began to get away with more than we did when he was there.

He would stop by during the day and do all the things my grandmother needed to have done around the house. He never stopped bringing us potato chips and other snacks from the Frito-Lay plant where he sometimes cleaned. He always had something like that in his truck, and I knew I would always get a treat when he came by to visit. Daddy Bo was so handsome and strong. He reminded me of John Wayne. A black John Wayne. He was my hero.

I was the kind of child who loved to sit around and listen to grown folks talk. I enjoyed listening to the teen-agers talk about their boyfriends and about music and clothes. I wasn't around many kids my own age, except I did have a friend named Judy who lived down the trail in back of our house.

In that area, we didn't have sidewalks or paved streets. What we did have were dirt trails that had been made by people walking the paths over and over again. You followed a certain trail to one person's house, or you could go up a dirt road to someone else's house.

Judy and I got into quite a bit of mischief together. One particular incident I remember very well was when we poured sand, rocks, and other things into Mr. Springfield's well. We were having a ball doing so, laughing our heads off. Then we heard a truck coming down the hill. It was Mr. Springfield. Instead of running back along the trail to Judy's house, we ran up the road to my grandparents' house. We didn't think he could see us. I don't have to tell you that he did see us and figured out who had been messing up his well. See, this wasn't our first time throwing stuff down the well. When he told my granddad, that was the first and last time I got a spanking from Daddy Bo.

I felt badly about putting rocks and dirt in the well, but I felt worse about getting caught and knowing I had once again disappointed my granddad. I believe he had to pay Mr. Springfield for damages, and it was quite a big deal. It took awhile to get over that.

When I was about seven years old, it was abruptly decided that I would go across town to live with my mom and dad. My sister, Diane, had also come home from California. So I started second grade living with my mother, father, sister and three brothers. My parents lived in a nicer area on the north side of Tulsa. The schools used to be for whites only, but Oklahoma had recently desegregated the school system, so now blacks were able to go to some of the better schools. Eventually, the whites moved to the suburbs and went to the best schools.

My folks wanted me to come and live with them. Melva, my mother, would tell me about the great school near them, which had drinking fountains with cold water. I can remember seeing the signs saying "Colored" and "White" hanging over the fountains at my first school. Even though we could drink out of any of the fountains, I still hated those signs. Eventually, the signs were removed, but I never forgot them.

My old school, Paul Laurence Dunbar Elementary, was all black and the new school, John Burroughs Elementary, was integrated. However, by the time I got to the new school, there were not very many white children attending.

When I first returned to my parents, I really wanted to go back to live with them, and I felt as if they wanted me. My mother kept coaxing me to come back to live with her, my dad, and my other siblings. It was ironic, and the move was so sudden that I wonder, in retrospect, if my grandparents had discovered that I was being sexually abused and wanted to get me out of their home before it was generally known.

2

SOWING BAD SEEDS

I desperately needed to get out of my grandparents' home. I was becoming an angry, bossy, insecure young lady. After I had been there awhile, I began to be molested by a male youth in the family. I was so young that I do not remember how soon the molestations started, or at exactly what age. I can say that some of my earliest memories are of being touched inappropriately. I just knew it was wrong.

Like most young victims of molestation, I felt guilty, as if it was my fault. I wanted to tell someone, but I was afraid to talk to my grandparents or my own folks. I just felt dirty. I felt helpless and ashamed, but in some strange way I began to expect it, almost looking forward to it. I thought that it must be love. And the quarters my molester sometimes left in my drawer only added to my confusion.

He warned me not to tell anyone. Once he almost suffocated me by putting a pillow over my face until I almost blacked out. I know now he wasn't trying to kill me but just wanted to frighten me into not telling. So, I kept all of the misery and sick feelings inside, buried deep, sometimes for long periods of time.

I knew I needed to get away from him. So, with the promise of a new school, a new neighborhood with sidewalks and plumbing that worked, and new school clothes, I said, "Yes, Melva. I want to come and stay with you."

We never called my parents "Mom" and "Dad." We always called them by their first names, because that was what they wanted. It made me feel a little sad that we were encouraged to use our parents' first names when other children we knew used the more appropriate "Mom" and "Dad," or "Mama" and "Daddy."

Along with my clothes and toys from my grandparents, I took a lot of inner wounds and scars that I didn't know I had to 2516 North Cincinnati Street in Tulsa. With all the guilt, shame, and negative emotional baggage, it is no wonder my school years were not the happiest. It's no wonder I kept looking for a way out, a way to realize my dreams.

Immediately, my sister and I fell into competition for attention. I didn't know my brothers very well either, because I was so young, no more than four years old, when we were separated after my return to Oklahoma. Another little brother had just been born before I returned to my parents' home. Now it was Diane, Ennis, Jr., Kenneth, baby Gary, and me.

I realized right away that Diane and I were going to "bump heads." I wanted to get to know her, but we never really understood one another as children. It was as if someone had taken two very different types of children and suddenly locked them in the same room saying, "Okay, this is your family. You've got to love her, and she's got to love you. Now, get along together, and let's all be happy."

Well, we didn't want to be happy. Diane came from a California lifestyle, complete with a canopy bed, Chatty

Cathy and Barbie dolls, and pretty much whatever she wanted. I, on the other hand, was coming from "the sticks," with few good toys and very low self-esteem.

In addition, there was great animosity between us and the boys, who seemed to be oblivious to the concept of family. I was not a very "happy camper," so I was always trying to get my parents to love and notice me. I really wanted my sister's love and attention also, but even the contrast in our looks worked to her advantage and added to my feelings of inferiority. She was very light-skinned with keen features and little freckles, and I thought my lips were too big, my nose was too broad, and my eyes were too large. And I had sort of large buckteeth. I was very definitely not the cutest one! I kept trying to get my mom and dad's attention, to get them to love me as much as I thought they loved her. Looking back at those days, I know they loved us the same, but at the time, I couldn't see that.

It didn't help that other people made a difference in the way they treated my sister and me. People usually made a big deal over Diane because of her pretty looks and gentle disposition. I got the impression I would have to earn the attention or the approval of others, so I became a "pleaser." I wanted to be pretty, and I wanted even more to be loved, but nothing seemed to be working toward that end. Every little girl needs to feel love and approval, especially from her father. A young girl's relationship with her father will affect most of her future relationships, either negatively or positively.

Once I overheard a very traumatic thing that was said to my mother when I was about thirteen or fourteen years old. It was this question: "What does that boy want with Helen?"

I was singing secular music by then, and a young man had come to the door just to talk to me. He was interested in music, and I had records out at that time. He was a couple of years older than me, and I don't believe he was interested in me as a girlfriend or anything like that. But I overheard this close relative asking my mom, "What does he want with her? We know she ain't cute, so you know he must only want one thing from her."

I can still remember that remark as a dagger piercing my heart, a dagger of ugliness and unworthiness that I carried around for years. The only thing I felt comfortable with were my songs, so I began to dig myself deeper and deeper into music. Actually, I had begun to write little songs when I was about seven or eight years old.

My parents were not Christians, so most of the time on weekends they wanted some kind of recreation, some kind of fun for themselves. They worked hard all week and were tired of the drudgery, so they would go to nightclubs.

Once, when I was about nine years old, one of our babysitters turned out to be the molester from the time I spent at my grandparents' home. I wanted to beg my dad, "Please don't let him baby-sit us, please don't let him baby-sit us!" But I couldn't say anything because of the fear of being hurt, and because I didn't want to expose that ugly secret. I was so afraid that I held back the fear and hoped he wouldn't bother me because now I was in the safety of my father's house. I thought, "Surely, he won't bother me here. Surely, he won't bother me, because he will be afraid someone will see him."

My sister and two brothers and I slept in the same bed together, two at the head of the bed and two at the foot with our feet meeting somewhere in the middle.

Well, he came and took me out of the bed that night and molested me on the living room couch.

I felt so afraid and helpless, but there didn't seem to be anything I could do to stop him. My parents came home unexpectedly early that night while he had me on the couch. Sticking his head in the door, my dad called out, "Come on, boy, I'm ready to take you home."

My dad couldn't see me because the molester's body covered my tiny body. My heart began to beat very fast, and I really panicked. (Even now, as I write this, my heart is racing and there is a lump in my throat.) I thought if my dad saw me there I would get a whipping, and my folks would really see what a bad person I was and never love me. And I wanted so much for them to love me.

By the grace of God, my dad did not see me lying there, and so, once again, the molester got away. However, it must have scared the daylights out of him, because I believe that was the last time he bothered me. I don't know if my dad kind of picked up on something and stopped having him over or what. I just don't know. But at least I was safe for that moment, and at least they still cared about me.

3

Sowing Good Seeds

My parents, not being saved, didn't take us to church.
However, my maternal grandmother, Minnie
Hudson, did. Neighbors also took us. One lady nearby
and her husband—the Washingtons—pastored a small
church. I am sure their church building seated less than
fifty people. They would go around the neighborhood
and pick up all the children in their little station wagon.
At first, we only wanted to go because they would give us
treats after church, treats such as a candy bar, a banana,
or an apple. A big incentive for me, also, was being able
to sing in the choir of their church. Occasionally, I would
sing at Grandma Hudson's church as well.

Grandma Hudson was a woman of few words, a lady
who spoke a great deal with her eyes. I have been told that
my eyes look just like hers. Grandma began telling me
very early, "God's gonna use you one day." She always believed that God was going to use me to preach the gospel
and to minister. I remembered those words and carried
them around for years tucked away in my heart.

When I was about nine years old, I had a very definite
experience with the Lord. My grandmother's church was
a denominational church, the Church of God in Christ,
and they really knew how to praise God. They knew how
to worship, and I saw miracles and signs and wonders in

those services. I saw people healed. I saw people with no food in their pantries being blessed by others coming to their door and leaving groceries for them. I saw the laying on of hands and people getting out of wheelchairs. I knew God was real, and I knew He could be very important in my life.

Although my grandmother didn't know the Word of God as we have been taught it in recent times, she knew God for herself, and she knew how to pray. Many times prayer services were held at her house, some planned, others impromptu. I always felt the power of her prayers, and she prayed for all her children and grandchildren. Prayer was a way of life for her, and I was comforted in knowing that she prayed for me.

About that same time the lure of secular music became more enticing to me, and the entertainment scene grew more exciting for me. I began to imitate all the singers and groups I saw on television. From watching, then emulating, I moved to doing. I organized a group when I was in about the third or fourth grade. With Beverly Mason and Deborah Morris, two girls who lived in Tulsa and went to John Burroughs Elementary School with me, I put together a very good singing group. We won talent shows all over the area. A little later I organized a dance troupe with Diane, my sister, and two of our first cousins, Saundra and Cheryl Alexander.

One year, right after Christmas, we entered a talent show with an original dance number. We borrowed our brothers' cap pistols, put on their jeans and shirts, and did a dance called "the pony" to a song called, "Bend Over and Let Me See You Shake a Tail Feather." As we danced, we would "shoot" each other, fall over and die, then get up and dance again. That night at the Rex Theater we won first prize.

15

So music and drama were in my heart to stay. I lived to entertain people. I was also singing on Sundays at grandma's church and at the Washingtons' church. I knew music had definitely found a place in me, and I had found my first true love.

4

A SUBSTITUTE FOR LOVE

When I was about eleven years old, my family moved from Tulsa to the West Coast. Dad worked for American Airlines and was being transferred to California. My parents wanted to get back there—at least my mother had talked about moving back to California for years—so they were almost ecstatic.

We, the four oldest children, flew to California unaccompanied. It was so exciting to fly on our own. We were greeted at LAX (Los Angeles International Airport) by my Aunt Dezell, who was my mother's aunt on her father's side. She was my great-aunt, a devout Christian, and a fantastic cook. Her collard greens with cornbread dumplings, and her hot link sandwiches with lettuce and tomatoes were off the chain! I'm sure we looked like the *Little Rascals* and the *Beverly Hillbillies* all rolled into one. We were so bright-eyed at what we saw.

Aunt Dezell, the aunt that my sister had lived with, took us all to her home in Long Beach. Her house was so beautiful, and both her front yard and back yard were like gardens. My parents and the other children came out several weeks later.

Not too long after we had relocated to California, my Aunt Ethel Alexander, mother of my two cousins, Saundra and Cheryl (nicknamed Pan and Boonie, respectively), who were part of the dance troupe, moved to California. They would accompany my parents to the local nightclubs on the weekends. Aunt Ethel eventually spoke to a nightclub manager about me.

Mom did housecleaning and dad worked at the airline by day. They both did janitorial work at night. So, come the weekend, they headed to the clubs to see Bobby "Blue" Bland or B.B. King, or whoever was in town. The first time my aunt told the owner of my parents' favorite club about me, he more or less brushed her off. But she persisted. Finally, he agreed to "try me out" on one song.

In that nightclub, after I sang, I soaked up the applause of the patrons, along with their smiles, compliments, and words of encouragement. It was as if they actually loved me. That is when I knew I could do nothing else in this life but sing. The club owner raved about me and wanted me back the next weekend. There were a few more people in the club the second time I performed. Then he brought me back the next week, so I ended up with a regular "gig" and a standing arrangement. Soon my performance went to two nights, and eventually to three and four nights. I was booked for long weekends: Thursday, Friday, Saturday, and Sunday. I will never forget the odor of stale beer, alcohol, and cigarettes, mixed with the smell of cheap perfume and old dishwater. But I so looked forward to being there.

I was not in church anymore, because Grandma Hudson was still back in Oklahoma. I did go occasionally with my Aunt Dezell, however. We went on Easter and other special occasions, or perhaps when grandma came to visit. Or, we might go to see evangelists A.A. Allen or R.W. Shambach or others at tent meetings. But for the most part, we didn't go to church anymore.

So I wasn't singing gospel. I wasn't singing church songs. Back then, popular R & B songs weren't all that bad. The songs of the sixties and seventies didn't contain the explicit lyrics that began to come along in the eighties. Music was fun back then—simple melodies and tight hooks with soulful, ad-lib-filled vamps provided the recipe for hit records.

Other clubs around Los Angeles started hearing about me, and I began to work two and three clubs on a weekend. I would do two nights here and two nights there. I might sing one night at the Cotton Club and two nights at another club in the area. I was beginning to make a little money. So I put my group together. My sister, Diane, and my cousins, Cheryl and Saundra, had the dancing part down pat, but we needed some work on the singing.

I'm afraid I was a tough taskmaster. In fact, some thirty years later, my sister and cousins still reminisce about how I kept them rehearsing for hours after we got home from school until it was time to go to bed. I would give them their harmony parts, give them the steps, and give them their moves. I loved it.

Of course, we had to have costumes, so my mother and my Aunt Ethel made our outfits from inexpensive fabric they would buy. They shopped in bargain basements for little accessories to pin on our satin dresses to make them look different from week to week.

Eventually, Diane, Pan, and Boonie became my opening act, and then we added another girl. This was necessary to make a foursome, because, when they opened for me, we needed three singers in the background and one up front. The other young lady was the late Ruth Ann Scott from Compton. The city of Compton is where my parents eventually set up housekeeping after returning to California, and it's where I spent my teenage years.

Our group was called Little Helen and the Soulettes, and we did all the old Marvelettes, Martha Reeves and the Vandellas, and Aretha Franklin songs. We even did some James Brown, Wilson Pickett, and Carla Thomas numbers. I remember laughing all the way home after attending a record hop where the Soulettes were the opening act. Diane was singing lead to the Gladys Knight & the Pips song, "I Heard It Through the Grapevine," but halfway through the song she began singing another song, "The End of Our Road." The band members had the craziest look on their faces as they scrambled to get the chords right. That was so funny to us.

We began to make better money. Already at twelve and thirteen years of age, I was putting groups together and orchestrating and rehearsing numbers. I knew I had found my vocation in life.

When I was about thirteen years old, a record company owner and producer came into the nightclub. He heard me sing and gave my parents his card, which read: "Bobby Sanders, Soul Town Records," and included his phone number and address.

We were like, "Yeah, right. Bobby Sanders, Soul Town Records. Motown—*Soul Town*. Ha, ha, ha. He's a fake. It's not for real." Aunt Ethel kept insisting, "Oh, yeah, this is real, Helen. This is really real. We're going to call him."

So we called him on Monday, and not too long afterwards, met with him. Also, we met with some financial backers, an older couple who lived in the Los Angeles area.

They did not know a thing about the record business, but wanted to invest in something. So they invested in Soul Town Records and me.

My first record, "The Richest Girl in the World Ain't Got Nothin' on Me," was released when I was thirteen.

" LITTLE HELEN "
The Richest Girl in the World

It was a big hit in California and this opened doors for me to entertain as a "warm-up act" for people like Stevie Wonder, Aretha Franklin, and B.B. King. The first time I opened for Aretha Franklin, at the Long Beach Arena, we had gotten a phone call at the last minute asking, "Can you be at the Long Beach Arena…?" Of course, we could. We were not going to turn *that* down. I remember hurriedly getting myself together. My mom and dad were just as excited as I was—and I was petrified when I saw all those people in that arena, people who were waiting to see and hear the Queen of Soul. I was so nervous and, at the same time, ecstatic. I had big crocodile tears in my eyes as I waited to hear them announce my name: "Ladies and gentlemen, the richest girl in the world, Little Helen!"

The band backing me up were young guys who later were part of a group called The Parliament Funkadelic. My first song was "I Was Made to Love Her (Him)" by Stevie Wonder. Then, of course, I sang my hit record, "The Richest Girl in the World." I don't remember hearing the crowd's response, because I was caught up in a dream.

Mom told me later that Aretha Franklin came out of her dressing room and stood in the wings to watch and listen to me, but I didn't get a chance to meet her. Her husband at that time was backstage, and he wasn't in a very good mood at all, which may have had something to do with me not getting to meet her.

I was kind of disappointed that I never met Aretha Franklin. She is still one of my favorite singers. I did get a chance to meet Stevie Wonder, however, and we did a concert together later at Wrigley Field. When I met B.B. King, the great blues musician, he let me take a picture with him. He was very nice and very encouraging to me. I was only fourteen years old.

I remember thinking, "I have found my place, and I have made my mark."

5

FAME DOES NOT HEAL WOUNDS

After that, I went on to record another couple of singles, traveled some, and opened for more well-known musicians. I also did several local television shows and record hops for various radio stations in the area. Basically, I was honing my craft.

As my popularity grew in the marketplace, it caused a lot of strife and more jealousy between my sister and me. I was not very popular in school either. On the one hand, I had made records and appeared on television and radio. On the other hand, a lot of kids were envious of me, so my musical popularity made me unpopular in some other circles. A lot of times I had to fight my way to school and fight my way home because some of the girls didn't like me. I was teased and chased home at least once a week.

Looking back, I realize I could have had a friendlier attitude, and I could have smiled more, but I was pretty much the loner. I experienced a mixture of emotions, but performing was something I wanted to do, and if I had to fight to do it, then I would fight. I began to write songs and associate with musicians and singers, becoming a part of the Los Angeles music scene in the late sixties and early seventies.

My background group, the Soulettes, became very, very popular as well. I think their ages were from nine to twelve, or something like that, and they had their own distinct style. The Soulettes would come on stage and do three or four songs. Then I would sing, with the Soulettes singing the background parts. The numbers were choreographed to a T. We were in very high demand, so after a while I had this entourage of parents, sister, cousins, Aunt Ethel, and an occasional friend or relative accompanying me. I wish I could explain how much fun it was. It was hard work, but it was also great fun. Sometimes it was two clubs in a night, and sometimes three or four clubs on a weekend.

This was something I knew I wanted to do forever. I did not want to work at a regular job; I did not want to do anything but sing. I wanted to finish high school because I enjoyed learning, but I knew I would make my living singing. I wanted to be a star. I tried to emulate everyone I saw on television.

The women singers I really loved were Gladys Knight, Mavis Staples, Diana Ross, and Roberta Flack. I liked some of the guys, as well, such as the Temptations, Bobby Womack, Sam Cooke, and Donny Hathaway. I would get happy as I listened to these singers. They inspired me, especially Gladys Knight and Bobby Womack. Their gifts truly are from God. These are the people I "woodshedded" with. I would literally spend hours listening to 45s and long-playing 33- rpm albums. I would study the inflections of their voices. I've always enjoyed singers who sing from their hearts, as they did.

I received a lot of attention as I was growing up. Sometimes it seemed as if I got most of the attention. Time equals attention. The fact of the matter was it simply took time to go to and from rehearsals and gigs. Recording took a lot of time as well.

Like most children, there were times when I did not feel a lot of love. Looking back, it's obvious that we were a typical lower middle-class family that was just trying to make it. My mom always went out of her way to make us all feel special.

Still, it was easy for my siblings to think I was getting all the attention because I was always meeting superstars, or making recordings, or leaving for the clubs, or getting new clothes. (God forbid that you should wear the same outfit more than twice in a season!) It seemed as though I was taking more than my fair share of attention from my parents, and I probably was. What I was really taking, though, was time. I have to admit that I was a very bossy and smart-alecky kind of person. I used to try to whip my sister and brothers whenever they would get out of line.

Subsequently, when my mom and dad were away on Las Vegas weekends, or somewhere else, the younger kids let me know that "You ain't all that great, and we're getting ready to show you, 'cause Melva and Ennis ain't here." It seemed they would plot and conspire against me. There were times when they even pulled butter knives on me. It was the strangest thing. I never got cut, but I got socked a few times, and I would get in a few licks of my own. But there were a couple of times when some blood was drawn on both sides—a busted lip, a scraped knee, you know what I mean. Whenever our parents weren't home we would run through the house slamming doors and cussing. It brought new meaning to the term, "Wild, Wild West."

I remember one particular time when I kept finding my mom really upset with me when I came home from school. Diane had told her that I was hanging around after school with boys instead of coming straight home. For weeks, as soon as the bell rang for school to let out, Diane would run "full out" for two or three miles to get home ahead of me. We didn't ride the bus.

She did this so that, if my mom was home, she could tell her that I was messing up. When I would get home, I would be in all kinds of trouble. One day I realized that Diane had to be running home from school and telling lies about me. So the next day I took another route and ran home. When she got there, out of breath, I was already there, out of breath. We had an altercation about that, as I guess you can imagine. Everything was out in the open, and I was able to tell my mom, "This girl is running home from school and I'm walking. That's why I'm not getting home when she does. Okay?"

Looking back, it's kinda funny. Diane did have a mischievous side. To be honest, all of my siblings were pretty hilarious. We were sometimes referred to as the "wild bunch."

My sister Diane and I have come to terms on a few things, and we talk and laugh about our childhood experiences from time to time. I love her deeply. We aren't very demonstrative and we don't talk often, but I know she's got my back and I've got hers, as well.

My heart's desire is to get Diane and my cousin Cheryl back into the studio with Saundra and me. Ruth Anne went to be with the Lord in July 2004. Saundra sings on some of my albums and backs me up when I travel from time to time. I want us all singing under the same umbrella, the umbrella of the Gospel of Jesus Christ, singing together for His glory. I pray it will come to pass.

My brothers and I are closer today as well. Today, the sibling rivalry continues, but now it is a healthier competition. My desire is to see them all saved and living for Jesus. All I can do is let them know that the same Jesus who loves me, loves them, and He is no respecter of persons. I try to let them know that, if they turn their lives over to Him, He will do for them what He has done for me. I see God moving in my family. Two of my five brothers are now born again. Hallelujah! I thank God, that, although we went through many trials, we have lived through them. Now, at least, we are able to talk about a few things.

Having a lot of emotional scars and carrying a lot of emotional weight from the past didn't help my attitude. Now that I know more about molestation victims, I can see that no matter what my family did, or didn't do, I would never have felt truly loved. As a young person, I was always on the edge, and I took everything out on those around me. I was an overly sensitive brat with an inferiority complex that made me difficult to be around and even harder to understand.

6

REAPING THE
BAD HARVEST

As I grew into my early teen years, the seed of the painful secret of my childhood began to bring forth fruit. The wound of sexual abuse was being watered by not experiencing the fatherly love and compassion little girls need most. Looking back, I know my father loved me. He was just unable to show it. In my day, we were supposed to know we were loved because our parents worked to feed us and put a roof over our heads and clothes on our backs. My parents worked endless hours so we could have the bare necessities. Nevertheless, I longed to be hugged, or to hear "I love you," or some kind of affirmation, but it never came.

All of this opened the door for promiscuity, which only fueled the anxiety and the low self-esteem I experienced. I ended up, as most such victims do, looking for affection, looking for love, looking for someone to say that I was okay. I was looking for validation.

Also, as is typical, I started looking for those answers in the wrong people. Band members in the nightclubs—some of them were older than my father—would "hit on me." And I thought that was real love. If anyone said the "right words," a kind word, or paid me any small compliment at all, I would immediately interpret their comments as love and acceptance.

I would skip school sometimes just to hang out, smoking cigarettes and "making out" with someone who had said "the right thing" at the right time. By the time I was sixteen years old, I found myself pregnant.

The circumstances that led to my pregnancy sound impossible, weird, "off the wall," and untrue, but they are very true. I became pregnant without having full intercourse. I had a crush on my best friend Bonnie's older brother, and he took us to a drive-in movie one night. He later sent Bonnie to the concession stand. While she was gone for a short time we had a brief "make out" session, which resulted in me being pregnant at age sixteen.

I kept it secret for almost five months, continuing life as usual. I kept singing in the clubs. I kept going to school. I kept taking care of my younger sister and brothers, but I knew something was wrong. I knew intuitively that I was pregnant. I kept hoping that my period would start eventually, but it never did. I was filled with sadness and fear for months. When I told my girlfriend about it, she told my parents. My mother was extremely upset, and I was called every name in the book—"You're this, and you're that...."

I could not understand how I could be pregnant, because this boy and I really didn't go all the way. We didn't have sex. Up to this time, I would only go so far with guys, kissing and touching and the like, and then pull away. I never went as far as I did this night at the drive-in, however. I thought we were safe, because we did keep our underwear on. It was what kids did... and it was okay, or so I thought. But I actually became pregnant without penetration.

Abortions had just become legal, so Melva wanted me to have one and took me to the doctor. The doctor discovered that, technically, I was still a virgin. My hymen was still intact, so he had to use some kind of instrument to break the membrane in order to be able to do a vaginal examination. My mother was asked to sign a release, giving permission to the doctor to perform the minor surgical procedure. I felt anger, disgust, and relief at the same time. I hadn't had sex, but I was still pregnant. Only then did my mom believe me. It felt as if a cruel joke was being played on me.

Even the young man didn't believe it was his child, and he kept saying, "Well, we didn't really do anything. It can't be mine." And I kept saying, "Yeah, I know we didn't do anything!" I knew we had come as close as I had ever come to actual intercourse, but we both were sure that I could not possibly be pregnant. For about thirty days my life was in turmoil. His parents and my parents would get together and talk. Then we would all get together and talk. They were discussing whether we should marry or not, especially after they found out I was too far along to have an abortion.

The young man didn't want to get married, which was cool with me. But at the time, it was devastating, because it was all so scary. Even though I, too, didn't want to marry, his refusal felt like rejection, and rejection hurt. My parents were telling me I had to get married. If I didn't get married, what would grandma think? In retrospect, I'm so grateful that we didn't compound the problem with a loveless, shotgun-style marriage.

The next series of events were even worse than all the previous ones: I found myself in a home for unwed mothers. My parents put me there because they couldn't afford to pay for the prenatal care—or the birth. They knew I could get some kind of assistance from welfare if they put me there. Then, of course, I would be out of sight, and out of sight, out of mind. At first, neighbors and close acquaintances thought I was back in Oklahoma visiting relatives or whatever, but I believe they suspected the truth—Little Helen is pregnant.

The worst day of my life, up to that time, was the day when I went into that home, which was run by the Salvation Army. I arrived with my little bag, and my little belly was sticking out. I was put in a room with just a bed, bare walls, and a sink. I ate cafeteria-style with a bunch of other girls who were pregnant—some of them scared little girls much younger than me—just eleven and twelve years old. They were little baby girls having babies.

They also took away my name. Whenever I got a phone call, it was, "Helen L., you have a phone call." The whole situation was very humiliating, especially when I became the subject of gossip in the clubs and at school. People began to ask if I were pregnant. I felt as if my career was over. I knew my family was ashamed of me. I, too, was ashamed. I cried a lot during those days.

From being a local child star, suddenly I was outwardly humiliated, the way I had always felt inwardly. I went from making good money to being on welfare. In addition, a representative of the home was "in my face" almost every day talking about adoption. I wasn't going to have my baby adopted! It was a dreadful situation in every respect.

The brightest day of my stay there was when my Uncle Eddie came to visit me. He was six years older than me and like a big brother to me. I begged him to talk to my parents and persuade them to allow me to come home. Eddie did talk to my dad, his brother, and I eventually returned home for a couple of months until it was time to have the baby. I returned to the Salvation Army facility about three weeks before I gave birth. My son, Jeffrey D. Lowe, was born on November 3, 1969.

Today, through my testimony, God is able to use what I've gone through to help other young girls. I have compassion for those who find themselves in the same position I was in. Sometimes just having someone to relate to helps with the guilt and shame associated with teen pregnancy.

Also, I'm not ashamed to let them know you don't have to have intercourse to get pregnant. It is dangerous just "to fool around," particularly today with herpes and AIDS and the other incurable diseases out there. There are worse things than pregnancy!

As odd as it may sound, pregnancy without full intercourse happened to me. There is medical documentation for this, and my mom backs it up. Sometimes it's even hard for me to believe. Whenever I share this part of my life—and it isn't often—it has a great impact on the lives of the young women and men in the audience. Some people want to scoff and say it isn't possible. However, medical research will tell you it is rare, but it can and does happen. I know. It happened to me.

Looking back at that time, I know the devil had struck a major blow at me. What self-esteem I had developed as a sought-after singer was now shaken to the core. This event was like an emotional, mental, and physical earthquake. It tried to take everything I had worked so hard to obtain. It took the self-esteem I had built and all my hard work and trashed them. But I'm a fighter. So I had the baby, a little boy that my mother named. When he was about three months old, I turned seventeen. When he was about ten months old, I left home and joined the cast of a road company of the hit Broadway musical *Hair*. I left Jeffrey at home with my parents, my sister, and my five brothers.

I wouldn't give him up for adoption. Then my folks thought it would be best to give him away to some family members to raise, and thank God I didn't okay that either. I fought to keep him in the immediate family, but I also fought to keep what I had worked so hard to get, which was my music. I loved my son dearly. He was a precious child, but I desperately needed to sing. *Hair* gave me that opportunity, and I had to take it.

The "earthquake" was over, and I began to build another life. The problem was that I was building on the same cracked foundation of hurt, pain, low self-esteem, and sin. At the time, however, this new life was like a breath of fresh air. Once again, I was in a place where everyone loved the way I sang, the way I danced, and they paid me "big bucks" for it. I thought, "I'm free, and I can start all over. Nobody needs to know about my past."

In spite of the traumatic experience of being an unwed teenage mother, I've never regretted giving birth to Jeffrey, although there were years when I wasn't a real mother to him and didn't take the responsibility for him that I should have taken. I praise God for everything He taught me during that season of my life, because it has resulted in something I can give back to society—an understanding. I've had the opportunity to support various homes, women's shelters, and rehab centers across the country.

I will skip to the end of my story briefly and tell the reader that I have been healed of all the wounds, hurts, and pains that I experienced. I am now able to lend a helping hand to some of the other ministries that aid young women who find themselves in similar situations. And I just thank God for that opportunity.

7

KICKIN' IT IN VEGAS

In the spring of 1970, about six months before leaving home to join the cast of *Hair*, someone told me about auditions that were being held in Las Vegas to become an "Ikette," a member of the back-up group for Ike and Tina Turner, who were at the top of their game. They were phenomenal. Theirs was the most exciting show I had ever seen.

They have long since divorced, and Tina has told the story of their relationship in a book, which became the hit movie, *What's Love Got to Do With It?* If you saw that movie, which ran in the spring of 1996 and can still be seen on television, or read her book, then you have a good idea of the kind of lifestyle I was about to fall into at seventeen years of age.

When I went to Las Vegas for the auditions, I sang Aretha Franklin's "Respect" as Ike played the guitar in their hotel suite, with Tina listening, and I got the job right on the spot. I was ecstatic and a little afraid.

This was the big time! For two weeks I trained. I rehearsed, I danced, I lived at the Hilton Hotel in Las Vegas and at the Turners' Los Angeles home. They didn't know I was only seventeen, however.

The Ikettes consisted of three girls who performed with the Turners on stage. However, there were about seven or eight girls who were rotated in as needed for the performances. As I got into the background scene, I realized why there were so many understudies, or backup performers. If someone was having a bad time on drugs, got fired, or was sent home for time off, there was always someone else to take their place immediately.

I wanted to be an Ikette, and they accepted me, but it didn't last long. An older girl I knew from the nightclub circuit auditioned about the same time as I did, but she did not make it. I have always thought she "squealed" on me and told them I was underage.

After about two weeks of intense rehearsing, Ike and Tina went to California for a concert in San Diego with Little Richard. I wasn't on stage, but I was part of the entourage. I lived with them at their home in Los Angeles for a couple of days before the concert.

While there, I saw Ike's other "old lady." Of course, they weren't married, but she lived with them all the same. Coming from my background, it was odd to see Ike with two women and all their children living in the same house as a family.

It was like, "Okay, no one's arguing or fighting or beating each other up. These women are just going along with the program." It seemed that everyone had an "understanding."

Ike, back then, had a reputation as a womanizer, but he never approached me. He never tried to make advances toward me. Whenever he said something to me, it was professional and it pertained to music. And I got along very well with Tina. It appeared that Ike had put Tina in a box, emotionally and even financially. He was very controlling. In fact, he controlled everything—the music, the people, and the money.

Once, Tina gave me her credit card and sent me downstairs to the gift shop in the lobby of the Hilton where we were staying. There was a particular purse she wanted, but Ike wouldn't let her buy it. So I got the purse, signed for it, sneaked it back upstairs, and gave it to her.

We got along really well, and I was having the time of my life. We stayed up all night. We could order any room service we wanted. I didn't see Ike and Tina doing drugs, but there were lots of drugs and volatile activities going on in the band and among the singers.

The girls would come in after the concerts, pull their wigs off, get high, and laugh and talk. For a seventeen-year-old, this was exciting and interesting. I just sat around and watched them, taking mental notes as the night went on.

Then one night Tina called me in and told me I had to go home. She asked me how old I was, and I wouldn't lie. She said that my being underage could get them into a lot of trouble. She sent me to the airport with my plane ticket and $40. She wasn't angry with me, but she was upset at what the situation could have become if the authorities had found out the Turners had a minor in their midst. Looking back now, I understand, but at the time I was crushed. As I walked through the backstage portion of the Hilton's stage and kitchen areas to get to the car that was to take me to the airport, I cried.

Not long after I was back home, I got a call from the producers of *Hair* in Los Angeles. It was playing at the Aquarius Theater. I had seen the show in January, 1970. It had been a birthday gift, and I really liked the energy, excitement, and the political statement the show made. Of course, I had always wanted to do something big like that, and this was the first Broadway musical I had ever seen.

The show made a great impact on me. Immediately I went backstage and very boldly asked the stage manager if I could audition. I didn't get a call right away, so in the meantime I did the Ikette audition and spent time with the Turner Review. In the fall of 1970, I got a call for an audition from the *Hair* company manager.

I sang a Jackson Five song, "I Want You Back," and I danced. The very next day, I got a call that I had been accepted. They sent me back to Las Vegas to get ready to go on the road with the first touring company of *Hair* based out of Vegas. They needed to expand the cast, because this company would eventually travel all over the country.

So a few short months after being sent home by the Turners, I was back in Las Vegas—at the same hotel, with the same band members, the same Ike & Tina Turner Review performing, the same Redd Foxx hanging out in the lounge, the same Sonny Liston in the lobby. I met the same group I had left before. Only this time I was not devastated with "my tail between my legs" as I had been several months earlier. Now I was back, and I was rockin' with *Hair*! I was able to go and see Ike and Tina and say hello to them.

The managers of the musical only needed a release from my parents, giving them permission to use me as a minor in the musical. So now I was legit! I was making more money than I would have made with Ike and Tina! What a victory, I thought. I was hanging out in the lobby with Sonny Liston, and "kickin' it" with Redd Foxx! I was having a good time—a little kid, just seventeen years old, out of her mind in Las Vegas. Okay? You had to have been there to understand. I was there, and at the time, that was enough.

I also had a chance to meet Elvis Presley. I had always liked Elvis, and was proud of the fact that we shared the same birth date—January 8. I was introduced to him by one of the girls in The Sweet Inspirations, a female gospel group that backed him sometimes. He said, "Hello," and I said "Hello," and then he—this Elvis Presley, this hero, this gigantic star—just grabbed me and kissed me on the mouth! A big, fat, wet French kiss!

I felt like screaming, "Help, let me get out of here!"

I didn't know what to do! I wanted to run. I thought I was cool, or "bad" as they say now, and I could talk a big game, but when that happened to me with this megastar, this superstar, my first reaction was to run! My origins in Oklahoma and the little California town of Compton surfaced, and I was overwhelmed. I kept thinking, "Elvis Presley just kissed me!"

I didn't think he was trying to "hit on me," or make a pass. I thought he was just trying to be Elvis Presley. I was this little, unknown black girl, and he was going to make her day. Well, he made my day, all right—and I made it out of there!

It was a good time in my life with my self-esteem being restored and finally doing what I loved doing again. We were rehearsing really hard and I loved the discipline of rehearsing. They gave me some very good parts for a beginner. After six to eight weeks in Las Vegas, we went on the road. We went to Hawaii first and then to about every state in the union. This tour continued for a couple of years.

Being on the devil's turf, I just kept sowing more "bad seed." I was introduced to drugs for the first time during this period. I was introduced to pills to go to bed at night and pills to get up in the morning. Of course, later that would open the door to harder drugs. Sometimes I would be too "wired up" after the show to go to sleep. I would be up playing records for hours, and some of the cast members would give me pills. They would say, "Take this," and I would. Everyone was mellowing out on Quaaludes and all kind of pills, such as Seconal and Tuinal.

With my low body weight, young age, and my system being as pure as it was, I think I overdosed the first time I took the pills, because I slept for two days. They did not call a doctor, they just let me sleep it off and made excuses for why I wasn't at work. When I finally did come to, I had to sit down or lie down every few minutes. So they finally gave me some "uppers" to wake me up.

Then it became a cycle to control my existence. It was "downers" to go to bed, "uppers" to get up, and alcohol, wine, beer, hard liquor, and brandy all day long, every day. And marijuana—marijuana was something I began to smoke from the time I woke up until the time I went to bed. And, finally, I "made friends" with cocaine. Everyone who needed drugs, even the thirty-year-old players in the show, learned to come to me at seventeen and eighteen. They knew I always had a stash of marijuana, or hash, or something.

I tried acid in Washington, D.C., and had a "bad trip." Part of me thought I could fly. Something on the inside of me kept saying, "Girl, you know you can't fly!" But I was in the window of my room on the fifth floor. Fortunately, I had the presence of mind to call a friend back in California, who talked me down.

The cast started to notice that I was "burning out" on drugs. Once I showed up for work high, and was fired on the spot. But the cast rallied around me, and said, "You can't send her home. Everyone else gets high. Even you [the management] get high. If she goes, we go." The show was delayed for a short time that night.

The cast wouldn't go on stage until they agreed to hire me back. Management did, and we went on stage and did the performance. That kind of thing didn't happen to me again for a while. Then I had another bad trip on acid, and I called my dad and told him to come and pick me up.

I don't even remember packing my bags, and to this day, I can't remember the trip home. One minute I was on the road doing *Hair*, and the next minute, I was back in Compton trying to collect unemployment. Subsequently, I had to go back on welfare, because my leaving the show was mutually agreed upon, and not a result of me being fired, which meant I was not eligible for unemployment. So welfare and food stamps it was.

Unfortunately, I did not learn from this experience with drugs. Instead of changing my lifestyle, I sped headlong down the same broad path to destruction. I became "friends" with a huge "snake," a major addictive substance, and my life went from bad to worse.

8

FRIENDSHIP WITH COCAINE

I left home before long and went to San Francisco for about five or six months, singing with cabaret groups. I was still getting high, still doing acid, MDA, whatever I could get at the time. I was still running around with all kinds of people—most of them the wrong people.

If the "high society" crowd had the drugs, I was at their mansions. If it was bums in the street or those living in the projects who had it, I was there. That is the lifestyle I had fallen into. Drugs—in particular, cocaine—had a hold on me.

When I was introduced to cocaine, it was like an immediate friendship. I began to get high every day on "coke." I snorted it all day. It gave me energy, a feeling of euphoria, a feeling that I could conquer anything, that I could do everything set before me—I could do it, and do it well. So I would run with anyone who had cocaine.

That's when I knew I was a hooked junkie. That's when I knew my life didn't mean very much. That's when I really didn't care if I sang or not. That's when I found out the drug scene could be dangerous in more ways than one.

I was with my boyfriend, Rick, one night at his place, when his brother, Nee, came to visit. We were sitting around talking, drinking, smoking dope, snorting coke, eating Chinese food, and just kind of hanging out. Suddenly, there was a loud and urgent knock at the door—BOOM! BOOM! BOOM! Rick peeked out, then closed the door fast, but immediately the young knocker kicked in the door. The next thing I knew, Rick's brother, Nee, was up against the wall in the kitchen, with the young man pushing a double-barreled, sawed-off shotgun against his side under his left arm. Nee's hands were high in the air in complete surrender.

The man demanded, "Where's my money?"

Nee yelled back, "I don't have your money, man!"

I knew that Nee had the money because he and Rick had just bragged about how he had "ripped the dude off." He had stolen $50 earlier that day from this guy, his best friend. The young man knew who had stolen it, and he came with a shotgun to get it! The conversation, loud and intense, went on for a minute.

"Where's my money?"

"I don't have your money, man!"

"Where's my money?"

"Man, I told you, I don't have your money!"

By then, I had run into the back room, off the kitchen, but before I could get the door closed to the closet where I was hiding, I heard a gunshot. Then I began to pray. I came out of the closet and looked out the window, but we were three stories up. I knew if I jumped, I would break something, so I quickly went back into the closet. It's funny what registers in your mind at times of crisis. I thought of Jeffrey, my mom, and grandma. I was petrified with fear. There was a little puppy in the apartment, and I still can hear the sound of it whimpering, because it also sensed the danger. The last words I heard Nee say was, "It's under the television, man. It's under the TV."

I could hear the young man with the gun run down the hall, get the money, and leave. Rick was sobbing, "You shot my brother, man; you shot my brother." We found out later that another guy was out in the hallway with a shotgun and a third man was in front of the building with a gun. Nee lost his life over $50. He was shot at point-blank range. The buckshot went under his left arm and into his heart, while he was standing in the kitchen. The pellets from the shotgun shell looked like red polka dots all over the white kitchen wall. He didn't have a chance.

After a few minutes, the only sound that could be heard was Rick's painful sobs. I could tell there was no one else in the apartment. I came out of the closet and called Rick and Nee's mother, trying to explain that we needed some help. After a couple of unsuccessful attempts to explain what had just happened, I blurted out "Nee is dead!"

Meanwhile, Rick was running up and down the hall, yelling and screaming, "He shot my brother! He shot my brother!" He was totally out of control, and I almost lost my mind. If I hadn't lost it that night, I surely almost lost it during the next couple of weeks as we went through the aftermath of the fatal shooting. We were back and forth at the police department, looking at lineups, filling out reports, and giving depositions as witnesses.

We would drive down the street, or be riding the bus or walking down the street, and see the guys who did it laughing and talking. Then we rode around in a police vehicle to point out the guys who were involved, which we did. I really didn't know what was going to happen next. I don't remember whether the three guys ever went to trial or did any time. I left the city.

I remember thinking a lot about Grandma Hudson at that time, "I hope grandma's praying for me," I thought. "Grandma probably doesn't really even like me anymore. I wonder if she has any idea what I'm going through?" I wanted to call my grandmother, but I was ashamed.

I wouldn't call home, because whenever I called home, I got into an argument with my mother and father, usually because I wasn't taking care of my son. They wouldn't ask, "How are you? I heard you just went through something traumatic. Do you need to come home?" Instead they would demand, "You need to come home; you're not taking care of your kid."

And they were right. I should have put Jeffrey's needs above mine, but I had so many issues that I just couldn't. I'm sure I projected a hard air of independence and self-sufficiency. I had built up walls to protect myself from the rejection I thought I was getting, and I'm sure the only opening they thought they had to appeal to me was through motherhood. It probably never occurred to them to say, "Helen, we love you. No matter what you do, you are still our child. Come home and let us help you."

My parents were as young when they had me as I was when I had Jeffrey, but they did a better job of giving me and my sister and brothers a stable home than I did with my child. However, at the time, I was wrapped up in my own feelings and my own life. I was too self-centered to be aware of Jeffrey's needs, although I really did love him.

But I didn't want to hear them fuss, so I would hang up. Then it would be weeks before my family knew where I was or what I was doing. However, I had a constant companion—cocaine. Human friendships changed, where I lived changed, what I did changed, but that terrible "friend" remained. Whatever singer, buddy, or girlfriend had even a couch I could use for a few weeks, there I stayed. Outward things changed—but the drugs never stopped.

One day, out of the clear blue, I did call home and got some good news. I don't know if it really was good news or not, but at that time it seemed like great news. The cast of *Hair* was getting ready to go on the road with another touring company. They wanted to know if I was available to come back to the show. I didn't have to audition this time. All I had to do was show up. So I got a ticket from Los Angeles to Miami, and I was out of the Bay Area!

Because this meant my folks could breathe a sigh of relief and stop worrying about me, they were very open and accepting of my rejoining the cast. I am sure they thought I would again be of some financial help, as well. So I was able to be at home for a couple of days to be with my son. A lot of promises and good things were said during that visit. It was a bittersweet time, because I loved my mom more than anything in the world, and she was talking to me as if she really cared about me. My dad was happy for me. I had been given a "wakeup call" when Nee died, and now I had a second chance at a good life with my family.

I'm sure they must have thought, "This is great! Helen's not going to be on drugs anymore. She's got her job back. She's going to be doing well. She can help us with the raising of her son. This is another shot at life for her, and she's going to be okay."

But, unfortunately, the drugs were not gone. They showed up with a vengeance as soon as my feet hit the Miami soil. I knew they would, but I was hoping that this time I would be able to control myself and my future a little bit better.

9

New Beginning, Same Ending

I was especially optimistic because I felt I was headed for a brand-new beginning. I felt I would be with new cast members, performers who didn't know about my past and didn't know I was practically sent home from the other *Hair* company after a bad drug trip.

I thought I would be with people who didn't know of my promiscuity, my insecurities, and my background. I thought they wouldn't know about my being raised in Compton and being an unwed, teenage mother. It was so refreshing to get on an airliner and leave California for Florida, where I could step into a brand-new life.

My illusions didn't last very long, however, and the opportunity to start over was short-lived. Actually, I ended up right back where I had started. I had just taken another turn around the mountain. A lot of the people I had known from the first touring company were in this company, too. There were some newcomers, but there were more old-timers. Instead of a new beginning, going to Miami was, in many ways, a reunion.

I got there and became very frustrated and disillusioned, wondering, "How do I live down my reputation?

How can I show the older members of the show I'm not going to be a headache this time? How can I make them believe I'm really okay, and that I've got a handle on my life? How do I meet the new members as a veteran, without the shadow of my reputation and rumors about my past hanging over me?"

Some of my fears and suspicions were warranted, but others were just that—suspicions and fears. Without realizing it, all my life I had been running from my past, beginning when I was a small child who was molested. I was running from feeling unloved, and I was running from rejection.

Just when I thought I could rest, I found myself running again. I was running from having a baby outside of marriage. I was running from seeing someone I cared about shot and killed. I was running from the memory of picking out the killers in a lineup. I was running from the shady people I had met in San Francisco. I was running from the memories of a lifestyle that I really hated. I was running to start over. I didn't know it, but I wanted to be born again. I wanted to be re-created as someone different. I wanted a new identity. I was running from everything that was bad and negative in my life, trying to start all over with something brand-new. But I couldn't run fast enough.

In fact, the very first night I was back with the *Hair* cast, there was a party with plenty of drugs and alcohol. It was too easy to lose my worries, frustrations, and anxieties in marijuana and hashish, in drinking and talking trash. I ran into my old friend cocaine. By then, some of the people had started dabbling in other types of drugs, as well. These were supposed to enhance your sex life by overcoming inhibitions. If you were inhibited, you wouldn't be once you took these drugs, or so I was told. Well, I tried everything at least once.

Even harder drugs were introduced to me at that time. And I praise God that these drugs didn't appeal to me as much as cocaine did. It sounds funny to me now, but that was really the way I felt. I would help someone else "shoot up" heroin, but I wasn't going to put that needle in my arm! I believe the power of God and His grace, through the prayers of Grandma Hudson, kept me from going the needle route. But the needle was what people were using more and more.

Here we were in this popular musical, which included doing a nude scene every night. After the show, we would sometimes party with a different partner. Some even held orgies. I went to one, and only one. It was just not my cup of tea. Not only did I have the wild, ungodly sex scenes to contend with, I also had hard-core, needle-popping junkies to deal with. What a miserable life! I wanted out, but I didn't know how to get out. I was no angel, believe me, but I believe my grandmother was praying harder and her prayers kept me from succumbing to harder drugs.

Looking back, I think we all wanted to get out. Some of us were worse than others. Some didn't do drugs as much as they experimented with the occult and New Age philosophies. Few things were frowned upon. Everyone was very open and forgiving and tolerant of everyone else's lifestyle and beliefs. *Hair* was like a community. Not everyone got high, but enough of us did.

Eventually, the cast of *Hair* ended up in Los Angeles for about a six-week run at the Aquarius Theater. I spent very little time at home with my family and with Jeffrey. It breaks my heart that I didn't spend more time with him, because he was mine. Yet I wasn't able to put his welfare ahead of my own. I knew I needed to be more of a mother to him, but I didn't know how.

After that, the show went to San Francisco, where Nee had been murdered. When I lived in the Bay Area, I literally didn't have a home. I went from house to house, from friend to friend, from stranger to stranger. Wherever I could find a place to sleep was usually where I spent the night. Whatever the price was to be there I had to pay it.

The second time I went to San Francisco, I didn't go as a homeless, drug-addicted, cabaret urchin. I went as a legitimate Broadway musical performer. A lot of people I had known before didn't know I had any talent at all until they came to see me in the show. Some of them, though, weren't really happy for me. Some were very eager to remind me of my past, of the things I had done with them, the escapades with which I had been involved. They were trying to show me that, simply because I was opening up a major show singing "Aquarius," that I still wasn't anything great. A part of me believed them.

"Remember? Just a few months ago, you were homeless," is the attitude some of my former acquaintances had.

My new beginning turned out to have the same old ending.

10

THE 'TRIUMPHAL' RETURN

I thought going back into the Bay Area was going to be a triumph, but soon I was hoping and praying the show would close early there so we could go on to another city. Eventually it did. I think we stayed there about a month, and then we went to Hawaii again. That gave me a chance to relax.

For me, being near the ocean is the most tranquil place on earth. I love Hawaii for its beauty, flowers, sunshine, people, and its proximity to the water. Hawaii gave me a chance to eat better, live healthier, and do fewer drugs.

It is difficult to get across to young people that doing drugs is not good, that drugs are the worst things anyone can ever ingest. But it isn't difficult for me to talk about drug use. I believe that if addicts can see that I was able to come out of that scene by faith in Jesus Christ, they will have faith to call on the name of Jesus for themselves and experience the same freedom I enjoy today.

What is difficult for me to understand now is how I allowed all that to happen to me. I continually thank God for the prayers of my grandmother, which I know are all that kept me alive.

After the run in Hawaii, the show kind of fizzled out. Its popularity began to wane. We had smaller and smaller numbers attending the performances, and people were leaving the show and going on to bigger and better things. We were not that exciting anymore, and people let us know that by not coming out to see us.

Also, America was entering a new era when psychedelic clothing, and "love children" and free sex were becoming passé. Before the show closed, however, I met Steve, someone who I thought really cared about me. I always was a sucker for anyone who said, "I love you." Those three little words were like magic to me. I listened to what turned out to be more lies and moved back to the Bay Area with him. It seems, even now, that the worst things in my life always seemed to happen in the Bay Area.

I thought being on drugs, being homeless, and seeing someone killed were the bottom of the barrel. Little did I know that the worst was yet to come, that there was a lifestyle that was even more degrading. Little did I know that I was really heading into the prodigal son's pigpen?

Steve was a former cast member of *Hair* who had left the show a year or so before I joined, so it seemed we had much in common. But Steve had discovered my low self-esteem and my need to feel accepted, and he knew just how to tap into that portion of my personality for his benefit. He ended up talking me into doing things I never wanted to do. If I could go back, I would do things quite differently. As the poet John Greenleaf Whittier wrote, *Of all sad words of tongue or pen, the saddest are these: "It might have been."*

This man conned me into giving myself to strangers for money to support our drug habits, to pay the rent, or just because he wanted power and control over me. I never really figured out why it was so important for me to do that when my singing could bring in perhaps $400 to $600 a day. In the seventies, that was very, very good money.

I never could figure out if he was on a "power trip," if he was having his own self-esteem problems, or if some woman had rejected him and he felt he needed to get back at her through me. I feel that somehow his attitude toward women in general and his envy of anyone successful, male or female, might have had something to do with the way he treated me. For whatever the reason, he had power over me, and I had a fear of him.

He gained this emotional power by alienating me, even more than I already was, from my family. I was made to feel as though my family not only didn't love me but hated me and was out to get me, and he was the only one who was in my corner. He also had me convinced that any value I had was through my body, or my voice and music. Not my talent. He seemed to have a fixation on pimp folklore, even though he was at that time a very talented musician.

He would say, "Go out and make money. Smile, strut your stuff, turn the trick and bring me the money." It was a game to him, a game that I hated to play. He would say, "You'll be powerful. I know you can do this. It's in you, plus, if you do this for me, I'll know that you really love me." In other words, "Prove you love me by doing this one thing for me."

Going into hotels and motels to meet strange men with whom I was obligated to go to bed was sickening to me. Sometimes I would get out of the car and cry, "How could this person who says he loves me, put me through this? This is humiliating!" Yet I kept doing it. Why? Because he said he loved me and I wanted to be loved even if it meant becoming a lady of the night. Where else could I go? I couldn't go home. I had been brainwashed into believing that my family didn't love me and wouldn't accept me.

I didn't even know what I was doing most of the time, not having had any experience with that kind of scene. I just had to "wing it." I was in situations that were dangerous, that could have cost me my life. But I know my grandmother's prayers helped deliver me out of a lot of bad situations.

Why do women believe the lies of men who have them do things that put their lives in danger? This kind of control by men is the same whether it is a pimp running prostitutes or a husband who abuses his wife. It is very obvious these men don't really love these women. "Love doesn't hurt" is an often-used cliché, but it's true nonetheless.

It usually goes back to low self-esteem, plus many times, there is a history of childhood abuse of one kind or another. Just as with teenagers who become pregnant, I now have a great compassion and understanding for women who fall victim to sick, misguided and abusive men.

So, at the age of twenty I was a complete basket case. I was a "zombie" under the control of a drugged-out person who was able to literally have power over my mind. It was a type of witchcraft. Otherwise, how could someone, in the name of love, get you to participate in a lifestyle you personally detest? It certainly wasn't love, but a psychological and emotional, or even worse, a demoniacal control over me.

I felt I had to do whatever he said in order to have a place to stay, to have food, and to not get beaten up or emotionally and mentally abused. I felt I had to obey him to appease the animal in him. Why did I not just pick up and leave? When a person tells you often enough and long enough that you have nowhere else to go, you begin to believe it, especially when your brain has been turned to mush by drugs.

You begin to believe it when you hear, "You're nothing, you're nobody without me. Your family doesn't want you. They don't like you. They hate you. They're out to get you. They never call you. They never do anything for you." Steve also had the bright idea of getting hold of the welfare checks and the food stamps my parents were getting for keeping my son. He concocted the idea that I was to tell my folks I was coming home on a visit and I was to ask them to have someone meet me at the airport. When my sister, Diane, said she would pick me up, I asked her to bring Jeffrey with her. I had no intention of going to my parents' house for a visit. In fact, I never left the airport. Jeffrey and I got on the next plane returning to the Bay Area. We had conspired to basically kidnap my four-year-old son so we could transfer the welfare checks to us in the Bay Area. No one but the Lord will ever know how badly I feel that I fell for that plan. What a fool I was!

Something I didn't know about Steve was that he had been in trouble with the law before we met. It had something to do with drugs—how did you guess? I never got the whole story, but drugs were found on him. He said they were planted on him, and he tried to sell them to a cop or something. For all I know he probably was set up. At any rate, the feds were involved. He had been arrested for possessing a large amount of cocaine. While he was out on bail, he met me, but never told me about the bust until it was time to go back to court. By then, I guess he thought he had a little robot that would come to see him in jail, and do things for him.

As soon as he turned himself in to do his time, I cried out, "Thank you, Lord!" I did so even though I wasn't serving the Lord at the time. I just felt relieved that the evil hold on me had been broken. By then, I had become anesthetized to turning tricks, so that if I wanted to, I could. If I needed to make a few bucks, I could—but most of the time I didn't need the extra money. I was singing again in a local band, so that part of my lifestyle gradually faded away.

With Steve in jail, I got up the nerve to call my mom and apologize to her and my dad for virtually kidnapping my son from them simply for financial gain. I asked if I could bring him home, and my mother agreed to take him back. At that time, and with the lifestyle I was living, it was best thing for Jeffrey.

I had been like a mouse that had been hypnotized by a snake, and now the snake was removed, and I was free to run again. However, there were still consequences to face, a harvest to reap, from all of the negative seed that had been sown.

11

THE WAGES OF SIN

I joined an interracial club band and began to sing around the Bay Area. I'd sing such Chaka Khan songs as, "Tell Me Something Good." Whatever was popular on the radio, that's what we did. My wardrobe was pretty much "out there," so I had the right look to be in the band. We were pretty good, but the drummer, Eric, was Steve's brother, the man with whom I had lived and who had just gone to prison. So the tie to Steve was always there as a reminder of my recent mental torture. It was always present when I saw or rehearsed with Eric.

I moved on with life the best way I knew how, which was to put up a good front, as though all was well. I did that by putting on high-heeled shoes, the shortest dress I could find, the longest eyelashes I could glue on, and the brightest red lipstick. Then I would go out and do as much drinking and cussing as I could.

The man who victimized me was incarcerated in Los Angeles and he wanted me to write letters to him every day. I am not a good letter-writer. I didn't even write letters to my mother or my grandmother! But here was this bum, who had done everything he could to destroy me, wanting a letter-writing campaign from me. For crying out loud!

"Write me a letter. What did you do? What have you done? What are you wearing? Blah, Blah, Blah!"

I was through with him, but I still wrote the letters! I told myself it was to keep him calm. Apparently, I wasn't totally out from under his power and control. There I was writing letters to a man who had almost destroyed me. I was trying to keep him from feeling rejected, trying to keep him appeased for just a little while. In the meantime, I was performing with this little rhythm-blues-jazz-fusion-type band with Steve's brother. Eric would give me a ride to and from rehearsals off and on.

Eventually, or inevitably, depending on your point of view, Eric and I became attracted to one another. I was still starved for someone to pay attention to *me*, not just my body or my voice. I think I fell for him because he paid attention to me. He made me laugh a lot. He seemed to feel sorry for me and apologetic for what his brother had put me through. So we began to hang out together.

Steve probably suspected something, because I slowly stopped writing letters to him. And when he called, I didn't have much to say. Then I moved into an apartment in nearby Richmond with one of my cousins, my aunt's daughter on my father's side. We were real party queens, and we partied all night. We cooked, we had people over, and we had Eric over. We had everybody over. I didn't care anything about Steve being locked up in jail. "Good riddance!" I thought. In fact, I hoped he was going to stay in jail forever. But he turned informant, and they cut a deal and let him out. Suddenly one day, there was another urgent knocking on the door, a replay of the time when Nee was killed in Rick's kitchen in a city across the Bay Bridge.

This time, it was someone who was after me—Steve straight from jail, or hell. Surprise! Surprise! Steve was about sixty pounds lighter than he had been before going to prison. I don't know what they did to him in jail, but I think he would have died if he had stayed there.

At any rate, there he was, knocking on my door. When I opened the door, my-my-my-my! It is a wonder I didn't have a heart attack from the sudden surge of adrenaline that went through my body. It was sheer pandemonium. It was confusion. He wanted to know if I was involved with his brother. He didn't even come inside. He just stood there and looked at me and Eric, who was standing beside me by then. The first and only question he asked was about whether or not I was sleeping with his brother. I should have lied, but I didn't. I said, "Yes."

Before I could blink, my front teeth were on the landing in front of the apartment building! Two of them—thank you very much. I began to look for them, with blood everywhere. By this time, I was hysterical. I had been through too much and seen too much; I had seen too many people hurt and misused.

I was standing there facing the devil himself and I had no better sense than to answer his question affirmatively. Then my teeth were somewhere on the landing in front of the apartment. Almost immediately I began to run. I don't know where I was running to. I don't know how far I ran before someone caught me. But I ran.

I was running for my life. I was running to die. I was running to escape. I was running to find my mother. I was running to find a friend. I was running to be hit by a car. All these things were in my mind. I was running to get away from the devil. I was running because I had no reason to be alive. I was running. I was running because it was the only thing I could do.

After a while, way up the street, Eric caught me. I had run and screamed all through the apartment complex, which was quite large. Someone had called the police. I ran out of the complex and was on my way up into the highway area—running and screaming hysterically with two of my front teeth gone.

By the time Eric and the police got me back to the apartment building, Steve had disappeared into the night, afraid of going back to jail. We never found the teeth, but I was too tired to care. I was too disoriented to look for them and put them in milk or water so they could be replanted. On top of that, I didn't have dental insurance and there was no extra money saved. I probably took some pills, I don't remember exactly, because the next thing I remember, it was the following day.

I suddenly remembered I had a gun in the apartment, a .38, and I knew I had to get rid of it because if Steve had come back, I would have killed him. I thought about killing him. I really did. I didn't think about killing myself. I wanted to commit murder, and I probably would have. The next day I kept asking that the gun be hidden. Eric took the gun and hid it. At least I was saved from committing murder. Grandma had to be praying.

A night or two after I had gotten my face busted in, I had a "gig" to do—without any front teeth. I went on stage wearing rhinestone-studded platform heels and put the head of the microphone, with its oversized sponge wind screen, right in front of the place where my teeth used to be. I don't know how I got the song out. I was on drugs and drinking heavily, so that I couldn't feel the pain or see the stares of the people. I had to work, because if I didn't front the band, they didn't work. My sense of loyalty, my show-must-go-on attitude, and my bulldog stubbornness were greater than my sense of pride at the time. So I went and did the gigs. And, of course, I needed the money.

Then I remembered that a year or so earlier in Los Angeles I had met a middle-aged white man who was going through a divorce. Before our move to the Bay Area, Steve had coached me on how to trick this poor man out of various material things. One of those things was a car. This man drove a Lincoln Continental Mark IV off the showroom floor and handed me the keys when I was just nineteen! He used to give me hundreds of dollars at a time just for spending time with him. Once he bought me $5,000 worth of sound equipment and put $5,000 in a bank account just for me, so in a few short months we had gotten money, a car, jewelry, credit card accounts, and the like. Then we just packed up and moved away to Richmond. What a terrible way to treat another human being! Now, here I was contemplating asking him for help—real help this time. I knew it would be a long shot.

I had wondered if I would ever smile again. I thought perhaps if I called him, he would help me. After all, he was one of the few people who ever helped me without using me in my entire life. I called him and told him about my dilemma, and he flew me to Los Angeles. He took me to the best dentist in the area and gave my smile back to me. I will never forget what he did for me.

I was ready once again to try for a new beginning. This one also would have the same old ending, but it wasn't drugs or sex that knocked me down this time. It was plain old greed, someone else trying to use me for their own benefit.

12

MEETING WITH GREED

I felt it was time to move back to Los Angeles and give up on the Bay Area, where I had experienced nothing but hard times and trouble. Eric decided to move with me. From the very beginning, I said, "This won't last, because it's not real." The only thing that kept us together for about three years was the fact that we had music in common. We could pretty much work the clubs together, and we got along well. However, there was really no love there, no commitment, and it didn't last. I lived only a few minutes from my parents and my son. Being that close, we could spend time together more often. I was getting close to twenty-four years old by then.

I signed with a group called Side Effect, and we did an album entitled, "What You Need." One song on the album became a major disco hit. It was entitled, "Always There." A couple of other songs on the album were "Keep That Same Ol' Feeling" and "S.O.S." The group was made up of three men and myself.

The doors were wide open for us to be what people were calling "the next Gladys Knight and the Pips." We had all of that potential in front of us. We had everything available to us. But greed entered in, as it does in a lot of relationships in the music business.

We had hassles over the signing fee and hassles over the issue of royalties. Jealousy also crept in because I was usually getting most of the attention—the girl singer usually does. Besides, I knew the game; I knew the stage; I knew the hustle. I had the stage experience, and I knew what I was doing and could usually pull off a good performance. After all, I had been performing professionally since I was twelve years old, and I knew every corner and inch of most stages. I had been taught every string to pull to get a reaction from the audience. I knew how to do my job. So jealousy, I believe, rose up within the ranks of the group and producers. I admit I was a little cocky. Finally, it came down to the point where I had to say, "Look, pay me my money, or we're going to have to do something else!"

Well, unbeknownst to me, they decided to do something else. They would rehearse with me during the day for an upcoming tour, but were apparently rehearsing another young lady in the evenings. One night I was driving home from somewhere when, on a local radio station, I heard my group, Side Effect, being interviewed by one of the local deejays. Only I wasn't with them. There was another girl with them, and they were announcing that I was no longer in the group. I knew nothing about it until I heard it on the radio! I sat in my garage, in my Lincoln Mark IV, and cried and cried. I was paralyzed with pain and humiliation. I cried like a baby. All I wanted was the money they owed me so I could pay my rent, get gas in my car, and put food on my table. I think that was the second time in my life when I came close to a total mental breakdown. I didn't know what to do, but God did.

Not too long after that, I got a call from a girlfriend who was singing with Julio Iglesias as a back-up singer. She told me she had gotten a call from the Captain &

Tennille's office and they needed a background singer. She asked me if I'd be interested in auditioning for the job. I told her as calmly as I could that I would be glad to. Inside I was quaking with excitement and anticipation.

So I got spruced up as best I could, put my best positive, happy foot forward, auditioned, and got the job on the spot. Now I was able to pay my rent and was getting ready to go on the road with a group I really looked up to: The Captain & Tennille. I went through about six weeks of rehearsals, paid rehearsals. Big money.

I felt really good, because now I could go shopping and do the things I wanted to do. Also, I began doing fewer and fewer drugs, because Toni Tennille didn't tolerate drug use. Of course, addicts can always find a way to do what they need to do, so I slipped around and smoked marijuana and had a little cocaine from time to time.

Certainly, however, I was doing fewer drugs and eating healthier food. Toni Tennille was into health food. She was a vegetarian, and I became interested in that lifestyle because I respected her so much. She is a beautiful woman, and she became a very positive role model in my life. After weeks of rehearsals, we went on the road, and I met a lot of really nice people: Dolly Parton, Hall & Oates, and Marilyn McCoo and Billy Davis, Jr., among many others.

We appeared on some of the popular television shows of that era, such as the *Midnight Special With Wolfman Jack* and *In Concert*. Getting ready to go on the *In Concert* show one night, I was very upset because the makeup lady had put this crazy-looking makeup on my face. I looked ashy and oily at the same time. It was awful. And I didn't want to go on looking like that.

Next door to me was a group called Rufus and Chaka Khan, and their guitar player, Tony Maiden, overheard me in the dressing room. I am very outspoken. I told the makeup artist I would do my own makeup and started to revamp my face. About that time, Tony came in and introduced himself as the guitar player from Rufus—as if he needed to be introduced. I thought he was the most wonderfully talented guitarist in the world, and I still do.

We became very, very good friends. He appreciated my talent and remembered me from Side Effect. He told Chaka Khan about me, and she also remembered me from Side Effect. There came a time when the group was going back on the road and needed a back-up singer. I made it known that I was very interested in the position. I got the job with them, and I was "pumped!"

After the Captain & Tennille tour ended, I began to rehearse with Rufus and Chaka Khan. I even went on the road with them while I was on hiatus with the Captain & Tennille. The problem was that I didn't tell my main group that I was going on the road with Chaka Khan. I was getting two paychecks. Wrong! Wrong! Wrong! I was getting a retainer from Toni Tennille and a paycheck from Rufus and Chaka Khan.

This worked until I ran into a management professional who knew the principals in both groups, and he let the cat out of the bag. I was so embarrassed. I guess I hadn't thought it through. I had become greedy, just like the people I had grown to despise. Sin makes you do some stupid things. That was wrong and stupid. Several times since then, I have tried to contact Toni Tennille through other people and through letters, saying that I would like to make restitution for the money I believe I stole from them.

I have not heard from either of them since. I pray that someday I'll be able to apologize face to face and pay them back. They were wonderful to me and taught me much about show business.

13

HITTING THE BIG TIME

After a very brief conversation with Toni and Daryl Dragon, the Captain, and their management, we reached a mutual decision to sever our professional relationship. This parting was very bittersweet, because, although I wanted to go with Rufus and Chaka Khan, I looked up to Toni and really admired the group's talents and gifts. They were an unusual group for the time, because they didn't look kindly on drugs and promiscuity. Although they weren't born-again Christians, they were living better moral lives than some Christians I had known in my lifetime.

If I could have had an open and aboveboard choice, I would have chosen Rufus and Chaka Khan anyway because of the kind of music they performed, and because I wasn't a background singer with Chaka Khan. I was a singer, dancer, and fill-in for Chaka when she needed me at sound check and such.

Also, their music was pure, raw, funky rhythm and blues, and that is the music I grew up loving. By contrast, the Captain & Tennille's music had a very pop sound—it was sometimes called soft or bubblegum music. By going with Rufus, I was able to get back to my roots, as it were. But I have always regretted how I parted from the Captain & Tennille.

Now, I have to admit that perhaps I let it turn into a dishonest situation because of wanting to get even for something that had happened a few months earlier. Toni had fired me without listening to my side of an incident that occurred while we were in Hawaii. Basically, they had an employee who, in my opinion, had some issues. He seemed to have a problem with females, and he definitely had a problem with black females who tended to be strong. I was all of the above. I was very black, very strong, and very female. So we clashed.

Sometimes we would get along, but most of the time we "bumped heads." Certain things were said over a period of months, back and forth, a little of this, and a little of that. I went through some biting of the tongue and a little looking away, and a little swearing here and a little swearing there.

Things came to a head when we were in Hawaii. My parents, my son, and two of my brothers, who were elementary-school age, were coming to Hawaii to visit me and to see the show there. This man did not do for me what he had done with the other background singers. He met the mother of one singer at the airport with a limo, took her to the hotel, and helped her get checked in. My people showed up at the airport and no one was there, though I had been assured someone would be there to meet them. Even a taxi would have been fine, because my folks weren't used to limos anyway.

Then when my parents got to the hotel, they had no reservations. Because there were no rooms available for my family, I had to move them into another hotel. The final straw was seeing my parents outside the convention center, looking through the fence, calling my name from the backstage area, saying, "We don't have any tickets!"

Everyone else's family members or wives had been accommodated, but mine hadn't been. All the months before I had bit my tongue, looked the other way, and gone to my hotel room and cried. Finally, my frustrations culminated in an explosion. I told him what he was and what his mama was! I told him what I thought about him, and I used some choice $80-words. I really let it rip, and I didn't bother to talk in private. Some of the fans coming to the concert heard me cussing out the guy. It was pitiful. Then Toni found out about it and wasn't happy at all, because they didn't look too kindly on profanity.

Here I was, this little black child, cussing out an employee. We went on stage and did the show anyway, including my blues number. Daryl, out of the clear blue, in the middle of a concert a few months earlier, had called me into the spotlight to sing a blues number off the top of my head. I actually had to make up some lyrics then and there.

Toni wasn't thrilled with him doing that, because, not having rehearsed such a number I could have blown the whole show. But I didn't. The blues number actually turned out to be a big hit. The audiences really loved it. However, even after I unloaded on the employee in public, and my people finally got tickets, they had me do the blues number anyway. The show must go on—big, fat, phony smiles and all.

I had assumed they would cut my solo out after the big blowup, but they didn't. They were consummate professionals. I did the number, and the concert was a big success. Afterward, I went back to the hotel room, angry, upset, embarrassed, and afraid. I knew I was going to lose my job. Sure enough, after we got back to Los Angeles from Hawaii, they let me go.

About three weeks or so later, I got a call from the man who had caused all of the trouble in the first place, and he was asking me to come back. I said, "The only way I am going to come back is if Toni and Daryl know what has gone on."

Obviously they already knew, or they wouldn't have had him call me. Toni's sister, Louisa, was also a background singer and had seen all the mistreatment I had gone through and, with Louisa's help, I was able to get them to understand that the employee had pushed me too far by humiliating my family. For six months or so, I went back with the Captain & Tennille. However, lurking in the back of my mind, I think I held a grudge and also a sense of insecurity. I thought, "Wow, they just let me go! You do one little thing wrong, and then you're history with them! No one even asked me what happened. They just fired me!"

When I was taking their retainer and rehearsing with Chaka Khan and Rufus, it was as if I was paying them back. Revenge is a terrible force. It makes you do stupid things. Of course, it wasn't the right thing to do. However, that is what my mind-set was then. "It's your turn to strike back, Helen," is what I told myself.

Actually, they were very fair people, as I had to admit later. They had a retirement plan in which a portion of each paycheck was invested. Several months after my second termination, I received a nice, hefty check for monies that had accumulated in that plan for me. Even after all the things I had done, they sent me that money. I didn't know they were putting this money aside, so they didn't have to send it to me. That is when I tried to let them know I wanted to pay the retainer back to them, but

I never heard from them again. I don't really blame them. Even to this day, I carry the guilt of my selfish actions. I learned a hard lesson. Integrity is crucial to developing lasting relationships in life, whether they be personal or professional. I believe I'll have the opportunity to do the right thing by them someday.

After that I went on the road with Chaka Khan and Rufus. We had rehearsed some in Los Angeles and then went on to Houston for our first gig at the Summit. Heatwave and a female group called Star Guard were our opening acts.

This was the farewell tour for Chaka and Rufus; they were about to part ways. And there was an opening for me to take her place, I thought. It hadn't been talked about yet, but the undercurrent was that I might be the successor to Chaka Khan, as she was going off to pursue a solo career. In Houston, we were rehearsing and everything was fine. We went shopping, buying all kinds of ridiculous, wild, and crazy clothes. It was so cool, so rhythm and blues, and so liberating. Everybody was checking everyone else out. That is when I first met James Baylor, or JB, as everyone called him.

I got off the bus at the Summit in Houston all cocky, knowing it all, and one of the guys on the light crew for Heatwave, whom I hadn't seen before, walked by. For some reason, he caught my attention. I don't know what it was that made him stand out in the crowd to me, except that God knew what He was doing—even when I was yet in my sin. He knew this was the man with whom I would spend the rest of my life. I just wished He had given me a "heads-up" on some of the details.

14

THE HARDER YOU FALL

After a couple of weeks of glances and hellos, James and I got together one night in Chicago, and we began to hang out and talk about music. We sat around in his hotel room smoking weed and talking about old records, and finding out a little bit about each other. He was very likable, very intelligent, and very, very soft-spoken, a gentle person.

He was also selling drugs, which didn't "compute" to me. This man, a soft, gentle spirit, intelligent, college-educated, wasn't like most of the men I had known in my life. He didn't fit the image of a drug dealer, or even a heavy drug user.

However, he was selling big-time drugs and had connections. All of a sudden, I was getting all the cocaine I could ingest. Free! Getting enough to give to anyone else who wanted some, too. Basically, I was misusing the friendship. But, ultimately, everything costs you something. He was misusing the friendship, too, of course. So we had this relationship on the road—a drug dealer and a drug addict hooked up together. Yet, neither of our hearts' desire were to sell drugs or to be users. Our hearts were just looking for love, for acceptance. We wanted to be important. We found that with each other, even though we centered it around drug use and rock & roll at first.

Working with Chaka Khan and Rufus was the pinnacle for me, with the exception of being a thirteen-year-old recording artist working with greats like Stevie Wonder and B.B. King. Chaka Khan was and still is a musical giant to me. She was fascinating to hear, and I loved to watch her perform.

Heatwave would open for us each night. Chaka would take the stage with such soul and vocal range that her performance was electric. I learned so much from her.

Every stadium and hall was filled to capacity. Famous people in other fields came backstage to meet us, and we had the red carpet rolled out wherever we went. I experienced the life of a star, like being able to get into famous nightclubs in New York without having to stand in line. This was the epitome of success to me—having everything you wanted at your fingertips, or at least only a phone call away. Success was living in hotels like the Waldorf-Astoria and being able to go where you wanted at all hours of the day and night. It was having limos at your disposal anytime. It was being able to pretty much afford whatever you wanted, or being able to talk someone into giving it to you if you couldn't afford it.

At twenty-five, I had everything in the palms of my hands. I had been through so much in my short life that I thought I could handle anything else that would present itself. I thought I was much wiser than my years.

Show business is such a powerful entity in itself. There is a very seductive headiness and sense of power about being part of the who's who in the world and being exposed to the kind of money and fame that it generates. Then there was the false sense of security and the false sense of hope the drugs gave me.

It was like a "triple-whammy," and I had no idea I was being set up for one of the biggest falls of my life. I thought I had everything under control. I didn't see any of it coming. When I fell I knew that there was going to be only one way out of the ultimate pit, and that was God's way. But I wasn't ready. With Rufus and Chaka Khan, we did most of the major cities in the United States. However, it wasn't like it had been with the Captain & Tennille, where we might do three weeks on the road and then have one or two weeks at home. We had months at a time out there on the road living this crazy lifestyle.

It seemed as if every week the momentum became more and more fierce. There were more parties, and more nightclubbing, and of course we always had the drugs. Week after week after week, I found myself trying to keep up with the others. I tried to out-drink, out-smoke, and out-talk everyone—including the men.

As the tour progressed, however, JB and I began to spend more and more time together. It became clear to everyone on the tour that we were becoming an item, as it were. A lot of times, we wouldn't even go to the nightclubs with the rest of the gang. We would go back to the hotel room and try to live normally, watch a movie and space out, or just go to bed like normal people do.

I think partly we did this because of our family backgrounds. James wasn't raised to be a rowdy, drug-dealing maniac anymore than I was raised to be a rowdy drug-addicted nut case. James had come from a lower-middle-class neighborhood in Cleveland, with his mom, stepdad, and his brother, Frank, who is about two years older than him. The two had been Boy Scouts and churchgoers. Every now and then, I could see that we were both struggling with the way we were living. I could see we wanted so much to be normal people. I think that basic desire is why we gravitated to one another and stayed together.

In fact, I think if I hadn't had his friendship on the road, I might not have made it. I think he kept me centered in an odd sort of way, even with the drugs and everything, and I believe I did the same for him. There were always people trying to misuse him, to take advantage of him, and I was the one with the discernment to see it, and say, "No, those people have to go." Likewise, I always had other men around me, but there was a kind of peace about JB that didn't cause him to get possessive and unruly when other men came in and out of my life. On the other hand, if some girl would show up and try to get close to him or hang around him, I got rid of her immediately!

I don't know how, but we made it through those times. There were times when I was so drunk, or so "out of it" on drugs, that I didn't know what city we were in. It seemed, also, as if I were regressing. I could see my teen years coming back. I began to feel as I had when I was traveling with *Hair*, yet here I was twenty-five years old. I could see I really hadn't grown up as much as I thought I had.

I remember calling Grandma Hudson quite a bit during this time of my life, just to see how she was doing. Also, I called home a lot more during the time I was with Chaka Khan and Rufus. My mom and I became closer than we had ever been. She loved Chaka Khan and Rufus. You would have thought she was the teenager, the way she loved all of their hits.

I spent more time with my son, Jeffrey, when I was home than I had in earlier years. I sent money home more often than I had before. Also, my dad was always there for me at that time. Probably the most important thing I had going for me, however, was that my grandmother was always praying. Before we ended every phone conversation, she would go to the "throne room" praying, "Father, in the name of Jesus, I thank you for my granddaughter. I thank you for the blood of Jesus that covers her. I plead the blood of Jesus over her right now."

My roots with my mom and dad and my son, Jeffrey, and having a friendship with JB, like it was, and being able to have prayer and unconditional love from my grandmother, I think, is what kept me from going over the edge. However, I was on the brink of losing it all. There were periods on the road when we laughed and had beautiful times, and then there were sad times. Once we got news that someone in the show had passed away. Although we were out there making big money, doing major drugs, living larger than life—we were human. So we had some good days, and we had some bad days.

Finally, the show was over, and we left the road. Our last show was in South Carolina. Rufus and Chaka Khan had gone home a couple of days earlier, but because Heatwave was continuing the tour, and JB was with the group, I stayed out on the road a few days longer. Then I got home to find that I hadn't paid my rent in a couple of months, so I was being evicted.

15

KNOCKING AT DEATH'S DOOR

By the time James got off the road with Heatwave, we had decided to live together in his apartment over a recording studio in West Los Angeles. That is when the drug life seemed less and less fun to me. People were showing up and knocking on the door, and his phone was ringing off the hook with people saying, "I'm going to come by and pick up an ounce or a half pound," or "I'm going to come by and drop off this or that."

Not only was there cocaine for sale but there was marijuana, and there was Thai sticks or hashish, or whatever. It didn't seem like such a glamorous existence anymore. It started to become tedious to me, and more than that, it was a little scary. The good-time life wasn't all it was "cracked up to be." Excuse the pun.

My health had begun to fail. I had developed ulcers from not eating properly and not sleeping and resting properly. I had developed sinus problems from snorting coke to the point where sometimes I would wake up in the middle of the night to find my nose bleeding. Once there was blood all over the wall where I had sleepily wiped my bloody hands. That was a very frightening, confusing, and sad time. I felt so trapped, so helpless. So sick.

I felt like the world was closing in on me, and I didn't know where to go. I had been advised to eat bland food, and my doctor ordered upper and lower GI x-rays to get to the root of the problem. I had been eating the wrong foods—fatty, greasy foods—and hanging out all night drinking Tequila, partying, taking pills to offset the cocaine, and hallucinogens to get in the mood, so consequently my health was wrecked.

I will never forget the night a young man called Cuz who lived in the same building in another studio apartment came to see how we were doing. Perhaps he was more than casually concerned. He had been on the road with Heatwave as one of the "roadies." He made sure all the equipment was off-loaded when the group arrived at their destination and on-loaded after the date was over. He was one of JB's good friends. They roomed together when I wasn't along.

He wasn't real happy about JB and me becoming close. One night on the road, he had become so upset about our friendship that he picked a fight with me. I had learned some karate when I was about nineteen or twenty, and a lot of it I remembered, so while JB protested our roughhousing, I kind of messed him up a little. In a way, it was funny—a little 125-pound black girl beating up an overweight, 250-pound white guy. But I never will forget the words he said that night in our apartment after he came in and got a good look at me.

He said, "I am here witnessing the demise of Helen Lowe."

Even in my drug-addicted state, my body wracked with pain, trying to keep myself together and keep my cool, but really falling apart on the inside, I knew what he was saying was true. I knew I was dying right before everyone's eyes. I was dying! In fact, my family members had begun to wonder how long I was going to be around.

"Is she still here? Have you talked to Helen? How is she doing? Well, I give her a week. I give her a month. Well, she's not doing too well. We might find her OD'd." Those kinds of remarks were beginning to circulate within my family, and the word would get back to me. I was basically a laughingstock, a pitiful sight. I don't think people knew what to do with me or about me. I believe my family wanted to help, but didn't know how. I could sense all hell around me. Of course, that is exactly what the devil wanted—for me to lose my life. That, I think, was the beginning of the end of the old Helen Lowe.

I didn't stop doing drugs immediately, I didn't stop partying, and I didn't stop dancing all night. But the words of that young man never left my mind. I think they were the catalyst for me to begin asking for help from a spiritual source.

"God, if you're really there, help me. I need to know you're really there. I know I'm messing up, and I know that I'm getting ready to die—but I don't want to die. And I'm not going to die! But, God, you've got to help me." As I prayed, that feisty spirit came up in me, that rowdy Compton attitude toward the devil came out of me, saying, "You're not taking me out!"

I didn't thank Cuz for his remark concerning my demise. I think I got mad and rebuked him for making such a negative statement. All he was trying to do was help me—and help me is exactly what he did. I pray this book will get into his hands some way, and he will know the part he played in my being the person I am today.

Those words became the catalyst for me to start searching earnestly for God. Finally, I was desperate enough and in the right place for God to reach me. With my grandmother back in Oklahoma praying, fasting, and calling on the name of the Lord, God sent someone to our studio apartment.

This young, black guy with the African-sounding name had come to buy cocaine. Then, standing in the kitchen, right before he left, he said, "You know, I've been watching this black man on television on Sunday mornings. Y'all need to turn him on. He's bad. He's preaching the gospel. His name is Fred Price. My sister and I have been watching him. He's awesome!"

I thought, "You are buying cocaine and watching a black man preach? Something's wrong with you!"

In spite of that, I believe God used this man to answer my and my grandmother's prayers. I knew God was real, but I didn't know if He would do anything for me. I had prayed, "Help me to get to you, Lord! Find me, help me, do something! Find the way to get me to you, Jesus. Get me to you!" And He sent this drug-using man to tell us to watch channel 11 at 8 a.m. on Sunday morning to hear Fred Price preach the Word.

16

TUNING IN ON SUNDAY MORNINGS

We always pre-rolled a couple of marijuana joints and put them on the nightstand before we went to sleep. So, when we'd wake up in the morning, we could light up before we got out of bed and pick up where we left off the night before. The next Sunday morning, we turned the television on to watch this black preacher.

It was awesome! This guy came on the screen with his Afro hairstyle and nice suit, saying, "Welcome to Ever Increasing Faith…." I had never seen anything like it. The preachers I had known held onto white handkerchiefs, and they would pat the sweat from their foreheads and kind of sing their sermons. I never saw anyone deliver God's Word in such a straightforward manner before, and I was amazed. My mouth dropped wide open, but I was also skeptical. Were these people for real? I looked at the way Dr. Price's hair was styled, and I noticed how beautifully the people in the congregation were dressed. I said, "Oh, yeah, okay, yeah—right! Are these people sincere?" In my heart, I knew they were, and I knew the preacher was telling the truth. Finally, the show ended. I was relieved and said to myself, "Phew! Thank God, the show is over!"

However, the next Sunday, the same thing happened, and the next Sunday, and the next. We were drawn to that program. Every Sunday morning, no matter how late we had gone to bed the night before, no matter how many drugs we had ingested, no matter how bad off we were—some way, somehow, we would turn on that show, *Ever Increasing Faith*. We would turn up the volume as the theme song played—*"Evidence! Evidence! Does your life show enough evidence?"*

I would say six out of eight weeks we tuned in to Dr. Fred Price. Then I began to watch other Christian television programs, such as *The 700 Club* with Pat Robertson and Ben Kinchlow on the Christian Broadcasting Network. I really liked the way Ben and Pat interacted, and I liked the newsworthiness of their program.

God was using everything He could to reach us. I had Trinity Broadcasting Network (TBN) on all night sometimes. Then, on Sundays I would watch the late Reverend E.V. Hill, another well-known Los Angeles-area pastor and several other teachers minister the Word of God. I found out later that my grandmother had been praying for the Lord to send "ministering laborers into the harvest field to touch her granddaughter." God was answering her prayer.

I began to think seriously about the word Grandma Hudson had told me as a child, "God's gonna use you one day. One day God's gonna use you. He's gonna raise you up, and God's gonna fill your mouth." Those memories began to become fresh to me. So I began to look seriously for God. Unfortunately, I began to try to find God in my own way. I began to look for God through people who told me they knew God.

In my case, spiritual hunger became dangerous because I was being misdirected. I found out the devil also operates in the spiritual realm. Many people today are caught in the web of occultism, New Age-ism, and eastern religions. They are trying to satisfy their hunger for spiritual things. Like me, many were simply believing lies and counterfeits for the true and living God—counterfeits for the real Savior, Jesus of Nazareth!

A friend of mine took me to a place where they sold candles and all kinds of weird powders, roots, and herbs. The shopkeeper looked as if she was from hell. There was something about her, something evil. My hair stood up on my neck when we made eye contact with each other. She looked at me as if she knew I was on the other team, that God had His hand on my life. That spirit in her looked at me as if it wanted to kill me! My friend said to me, "Get this oil and put it on your money, and get this candle and burn it for relationships. Get this other kind of oil to attract lovers, etc, etc." I came out of that shop with a terrible headache and a sack full of devil stuff! I started burning candles and putting oil on all my money. Every time I paid for something, people looked at me a little strange because my money smelled of the pungent oil.

Once I went looking for someone who read tarot cards. My openness to all these ideas had been planted when I was in the cast of *Hair.* That musical was all about drugs, sex, astrology, and witchcraft. So, when I started to search for the things of God, the devil sent false angels of light—people to direct me to other gods. In the back of my mind, I knew Jesus had been born, had died, and had been resurrected. I knew He was the Son of God and that He died for my sins. I knew what the Word of God said. I knew what my grandmother had taught me. I knew what those old-time preachers in Oklahoma had preached. I knew what Dr. Price had ministered on television. I knew grandma laid hands on sick people, anointed them with oil, and God raised them up.

I knew in my heart that Jesus was the Way, but I was trying to find a Jesus who would be compatible with *my* way of living. I wanted to have Jesus and my own lifestyle at the same time.

Then I went to a psychic, because I was having relationship problems with JB. She told me some things to do, but when I went home, mirrors began to fall off the walls and weird things began to happen. I thought, "Oh, man, I've really messed up now. I've hooked up with the devil!"

I didn't know how I was going to escape his clutches! I also listened to psychics on television, like the man who said to put a glass of water at the side of your bed so the "sweet spirits" could drink it at night. I actually did all that stupid stuff! No wonder I was a basket case by the time I got saved.

The same man told his audience to write down what they wanted on a sheet of paper and believe they would get it. It sounds like faith, doesn't it? I had done that once earlier in my life, and it worked. When I was nineteen years old, I had written down a Lincoln Continental, $5,000 in cash, a sound system, and a lot of other things that I wanted on a sheet of paper and put the list under my pillow. Before long, as I mentioned earlier, I got those things, including the car! So, I knew the devil had power, counterfeit power, and was trying to get me, but I also knew I needed Jesus. I knew in my heart that Jesus had the real power, that He was my only help.

I watched Christian television off and on and went to this psychic at the same time. She was taking money from me. "Bring me back $200; bring me back $100," she would command. I didn't know where I was going to get the money, but I was afraid that if I didn't take it to her something worse might happen. Finally, something on the inside of me said, "I'm not taking her anything back! I'm not taking her back one thin dime. *Nada!* She can't do anything to me! Who does she think she is?" I believe that was God telling me, *"You don't have to bow down to the devil! Jesus is Lord!"*

Finally, I went to a place in Los Angeles where they had pillows on the floor. The place reeked of incense, and the adherents said, "Yeah, come on, Helen, yeah, come over here. You can get saved right over here and go ahead and be spiritual and live your life." They told me, "You know, so-and-so is in this religion, and so is so-and-so." I was impressed and still searching for an answer, so I listened.

They named all the big stars involved in that religion to make me feel comfortable about joining the group. So I sat on the floor on pillows, smelled the incense, looked at the fruit and beautiful flowers, and saw a lot of other people just sitting around. They looked strange to me. I remember they didn't eat meat. Everything had to be pure—although they didn't look clean. For some reason, they just didn't look clean.

They sat on the floor, and they began to hum, "Ohm-mmmm." I said to myself, "No, I'm going hommmmme. The devil is a liar! I know this ain't God sitting on the floor. I could do this at home—and at least my house is clean!"

By this time, I was also dabbling in Egyptology. I had pyramids and different kinds of posters and so forth hanging on my bedroom walls. I had all this evil stuff around me, including marijuana, drugs, evil paraphernalia, and pyramids in the room. Nevertheless, God had His hand on my life, and grandma was praying me through.

I thank God for my grandmother who would come to visit me, discern all of the evil around me, and go back home with a burden for me, and fast and pray. While she was with me, she would give me a prayer cloth, anoint my forehead with oil, pray and weep over me. Then she would go back home with that burden, and continue to fight for my soul.

She held onto God with one hand and me with the other, that I might not die without Jesus. She held onto the prayer that I would live and proclaim the Gospel of the Lord Jesus Christ. In May, 2004, at the age of 101, my grandmother, Minnie Hudson, went to be with Jesus. I thank God always that she lived to see her prayers gloriously answered. Hallelujah! Glory to God!

Back then, it wasn't just my physical health that was deteriorating, I felt as if I was literally losing my mind. All of that, I know now, was spiritual warfare. The enemy was trying to "take me out." A friend called during this time to ask me to audition for Julio Iglesias. I was so depressed, weighed down by spirits of darkness, that she heard it in my voice and I know that is why she cut the conversation short and never called back.

I was in the middle of such a battle! I was drawn to the occult. I was drawn to the supernatural, thinking that all spirituality was part of the same thing. At the same time, I was still watching Dr. Price, still watching Pat and Ben, and still watching Paul and Jan Crouch on TBN.

Dr. Price would teach, *"Faith is the substance of things hoped for, the evidence of things not seen"*—and I tried to figure that out! I was trying to figure it out in my mind. Can you imagine trying to figure out the Word of God while high on cocaine? We had learned how to free-base cocaine and had become really good at it. I had become a regular little pharmacist and could make some of the better free-base, which is what they call "crack" now. It was just a purer form of the same poison.

But I was making more and more free-base and enjoying it less. JB would look at me taking a hit, and my eyes would get big. Then I would watch him take a hit, and his eyes would get big. We would become too hot, although it was wintertime. Then we would walk around with no clothes on, smoking crack, with witchcraft artifacts and occult books all around us. During those times I wouldn't turn on the television, because I didn't want to see any Christians. I didn't want to hear them talk about Jesus. I also was operating in such paranoia at that time. It felt as if everyone was out to get me. I was sure that the devil was.

17

MY NIGHT TO DIE

One night, I passed out smoking the free-base pipe. When I came to, it was evident that my bodily functions were going haywire, for I was sweating profusely and experiencing uncontrolled diarrhea. Even before I passed out, I can remember standing against the wall, saying, "Well, what in the world!"

It was a total nightmare—demonic to the core! There were spirits all around me in that place. I was smoking dope, and that was my night to die. I passed out and never fell, just slid down the wall. When I came to a few seconds later, my knees were kind of bent and I was stuck to the wall! I watched JB take another hit. I took another hit, too! I didn't have enough sense to stop, and JB didn't have enough sense to stop me.

My heart was beating so fast. I looked as if I had just taken a shower from all of the perspiration—and I believe I was literally dying! My grandmother told me later that, at the same time this was happening to me, she was on her face in her little house back in Tulsa, crying out to the Lord, "Save my granddaughter," and pleading the blood of Jesus over me. I am so grateful to her today, for that was the night Grandma "prayed me through." (She later told me that she had been fasting for about two weeks, just taking water and praying. She lay on her linoleum floor, battled for my soul, and won!)

Once all the cocaine is gone, you dig around in the carpet for residue, for anything resembling a "rock." After you have smoked the residue, after you have put ether in the bottom of the pipe and swished it around, and poured it out, and smoked that residue, after you have coughed up black soot, after your lips have turned blue from ingesting that poison and you suddenly let it sink in that it is all gone—you have to go to bed. Only then it's daylight, and you feel like a vampire. I felt so helpless and so ashamed.

What would you do when there is no more dope, no more high? You would sell yourself to get dope. You would do it! At that time in my life, I believe that God had His hand on me so strongly that He wouldn't let me sell myself again. We had hocked just about everything we were strong enough to carry out of the place, but He wouldn't let me sell myself, and He wouldn't let me take anything else out of the apartment.

I know it was my grandmother's prayers that sustained me until I could come down off that trip. Later that week, I began to watch Christian television again. One night in particular, as I was tuned in, it was as if God himself rebuked the devil for my sake. I know that promise of rebuking the devil for our sakes concerns tithing (Malachi 3:11). However, I believe God can rebuke Satan any time He wants to in answer to heartfelt prayer. I believe grandma had gotten God's attention.

I believe He said, "Stop! Leave Helen alone! She is mine! Enough is enough!"

The power of God backed the devil off long enough for me to make an intelligent decision that night in my living room. That decision was to call upon the name of

Jesus. It was the most intelligent decision I have ever made in my life.

I said, "Lord Jesus, if you'll just take me back, I want to be free. I want to come home. I don't want to live like this."

As I sat there on the floor staring at the television, calling out to God, I suddenly remembered this little church at the back of our apartment building. I thought the sign had always read "Church of God in Christ," a denomination I had attended as a child, but it didn't say that; It said, "Church of Christ."

I didn't care what it was called! I looked it up in the phone book and called that little church. As it happened, the pastor, a middle-aged white man, was at the church, and he answered the phone. I told him which apartment building I lived in next door to his church.

I was crying and said, "I was watching Christian television.... I need to get saved. I need to get saved right now! Could you come over here, or could I come over there? I need to get saved!"

I know he must have thought, "Either this lady is serious, or she's crazy!"

The people in this particular denomination are usually not very emotional. Neither are they Pentecostal nor charismatic, and there I was "boohooing" all over the telephone. In spite of that, the pastor was serious about God, and he came over anyway and prayed the Sinner's Prayer with me. As he was leaving he asked, "Well, is there anything else I can do for you?"

I said, "Yes, I want you to pray that all these habits be taken away from me."

He asked, "What habits are those?"

God has to be compassionate, and He has to have a sense of humor, because I really should have told the pastor the whole truth and nothing but the truth. But I was so full of pride that I didn't want the man of God to know I had been smoking coke, and free-basing. So I said, softly, "Drinking wine."

I don't think I even told him about the marijuana. It was so silly, looking back, that I didn't want him to think badly of me. However, I knew God knew what I was talking about. I didn't want this man to think I was a "low-life," so I said, "drinking wine."

The pastor prayed that God would deliver me and set me free from the habits, but he probably discerned there were other things going on in addition to drinking wine. The miraculous thing, under the circumstances, is that he prayed with me and I was instantly set free and delivered from drugs—not just from wine, but also from marijuana, pills, cocaine, and the whole drug scene.

I was also instantly delivered from different types of music. There was certain music after that that I didn't want to hear anymore. I didn't care if you listened to it, but I didn't like it.

Things began to look different to me. I thanked the pastor for coming, and I wept and thanked God for him being there. However, I was starting to feel a little self-conscious and a bit foolish. Here I was with my sordid background with this man in my apartment praying for me. About that time, here comes my drug-dealing room-mate.

JB wanted to know, "Who's this man in my apart-ment?"

Immediately, the pastor introduced himself, and I talked fast to let James know what he was doing there and that I had gotten saved. He just looked at the man and said, in essence, "Well, thank you very much. You know, she really did need help, and we—we thank you for coming over. But I don't need any help, so I guess your work is done. See ya."

I remember sitting on the couch feeling free for the first time in years—free, just totally free! I picked up the phone to call grandma, but I couldn't remember her number. The devil was still trying to mess with my mind. He didn't want grandma to get the good report. I kept trying to remember her phone number and couldn't.

I had called her all the time. I could call grandma on a touch-tone phone in the dark, but at that moment, I couldn't remember anything but the area code—918 ...918 ...918 ... It was as if the devil was still trying to hold on to me.

My drug-dealing roommate thought it would be only a couple of weeks and then I would start doing drugs again, because I had quit before and started again. With a little temptation, and after a period of time, he thought I would be right back in there with him. However, this time the deliverance was real. It was Jesus who had delivered me this time!

I decided to call my parents to tell them the good news and to get grandma's phone number. They didn't seem too happy for me. I guess they were, but, perhaps, like James, they thought it wouldn't last. They didn't react as I had thought they would. I dialed grandma's number very carefully and eventually got her on the line. I told her I had gotten saved. Her response was all I could have wished for. She began to praise and worship the Lord. We had a praise service—long distance.

She told me then how she had been praying for me, and how over the past two weeks, in particular, she had been fasting and lifting me up in prayer. Everyone she laid hands on during the time she was fasting and praying had been healed. Miracles had taken place. We rejoiced and praised God together. We gave God the glory and the praise for what He had done in my life and for what He was going to do in my life. I had no idea how God was going to move in my life. I thought perhaps He would make me the next Mahalia Jackson or the next big Christian music-recording artist. After all, I had something to sing about now.

I said, "Father, I will never sing another secular song as long as I live." But it was six years after I was completely healed and delivered from drugs before He used me in music ministry.

18

Waiting Six Years for a Dream

After I was totally set free from drugs, I began to attend services at the church I used to watch on television on Sunday mornings.

It seemed as though every page in the Bible said, "Flee fornication." When I mentioned this to JB, he didn't respond favorably, so once again I was at a crossroads. "What should I do? Where will I go?"

I called grandma, who told me to stay put, that she would pray. About that same time, I found out that I was pregnant. I called out to God because I had learned by then that I was not to marry an unbeliever. JB definitely wasn't saved, and I was stuck. I wouldn't get an abortion, and I didn't have any money to support myself. JB and I were at a standoff. We hardly spoke to each other. I almost lost it and went back to the ways of the world, when one day JB surprised me and asked if I wanted to go to Las Vegas and get married.

We were married on June 5, 1981.

Our first child, a daughter we named Jovan, was born in October of that year. It was a wonderful time of restoration and healing. We didn't have the kind of finances we were used to from the music days, but James was working at Lockheed, a major aerospace company.

He still sold a few drugs on the side, but it didn't bother me, as long as he wasn't smoking pot in the house. To me, marijuana had become repulsive. He was still drinking beer, but that didn't bother me either. I knew sooner or later my prayers for him would be answered. Basically, my life had begun anew, because of the power of God, and the power of prayer.

When I said, "God, I will never sing secular music again," instantly, God spoke to my heart, saying, *"Sit down."* I heard Him say, "Sit down" on the inside of me. It wasn't an audible voice, but I heard Him just the same. He said, *"Sit down, and learn of Me."*

So, I regularly attended Crenshaw Christian Center, standing in line early on Sunday mornings to get into the sanctuary. I didn't have any nice clothes in the beginning. Some of my clothes were actually pretty ugly.

However, I did the best I could with my hair and my makeup. I remember standing in line during the early days with these beautiful people who, to me, were dressed better than the Hollywood stars. I would walk up to them in my baggy pants and my catalogue-bought sweater with my little Bible in hand and say, "How ya'll doing?"

Everyone would look at me, and say, "Blessed. We are blessed." Perhaps they didn't mean to, but it was almost as if they put their noses up in the air. It was almost as if they were kind of looking down on me. You see, I still had esteem issues.

So I said to myself, "Okay, they have their own way of talking here. They say, 'I'm blessed,' they don't say 'I'm fine.' They don't say they are doing 'okay' or 'well.' They say, 'I'm blessed.' Then I tried to say it, and the next time

someone asked me, "How are you?" I said, "BLESSED!"
All loud and country. BLESSED!

Immediately the Holy Spirit said to me in that inward
voice, *"Be yourself. Just say fine. Just stick with fine. You know
you're blessed. You can say blessed when you want to. When you're
ready."* So I went back to being "fine" and "well" until I
was comfortable. It was so funny.

I never will forget wanting to dress like those women.
The first thing I asked God for was pearls. I didn't ask
for real pearls, but a string of simulated pearls and a pair
of little pearl earrings, and God blessed me with them!
Then I wanted some dresses that fit me, and soon my
mom sent me some dresses from a lady she worked for.
There were several beautiful knit and silk dresses. Then
all I needed was shoes.

There was one particular shoe store called Standard
Brands where I had always wanted to get shoes. I prayed
and asked God to let me buy shoes there, and He did.
I got some black patent leather dress shoes that went
with just about everything. I felt really *blessed*, and I did
not have to say it as a simple religious response. Then I
went and sat on the front row every Sunday and received
the Word of God.

After a couple of years, I became an employee of the
ministry, and we moved from our little apartment in North
Hollywood to a big house in South Central Los Angeles.
Our daughter, Jovan, couldn't play in the front yard then
because of the gang activity in the area, complete with
bullets flying. But we had a big backyard, and we were
only seven minutes from the church. However, James had
to drive about forty-five minutes to work everyday. For us,
it was an easy compromise.

My first job at Crenshaw was as a tape-duplicator.
After our second child, James II, was born, I returned to

work as a letter analyst. Basically, my job was to read all of Dr. Price's mail, sort it, and route it.

I was so grateful to God for giving me a home, a husband, a family, and a house with a back yard that was only seven minutes from the church, and a job at the ministry! He also enabled us to buy a little used car that I didn't have to hide in the garage for fear of it being repossessed. I could drive and park it anywhere.

But not being able to sing for God began to curdle in my spirit. God had told me, after I was saved and delivered, that He had indeed called me to preach the gospel. Grandma was right! However, any singing and preaching were put "on the shelf " for a long time. After a while singing began to bubble up in my spirit again.

"God, I want to sing," I would say. "God, I want to sing." But I wasn't even in the choir at Crenshaw. It seemed impossible. I called Shirley Caesar on a radio talk show once, and asked her, "What should I do? I want to sing for God. What should I do?"

She said, "Start where you are in your home church. God knows where you are, and He'll do the rest."

That is exactly what I did. After I had been a member of the church for four years, I was allowed to join the choir. I wasn't allowed to sing any lead songs right away, though. Basically, I felt like just another "robe." I wanted to sing a solo, but I learned to be content. Eventually, I learned to rejoice in the fact that I was singing at all. Then I began to question God again.

After I had served God for approximately three years, James finally received Jesus as his personal Lord and Savior. It had been tedious living with him while he was not willing to serve God, but I kept praying for him. Occasionally, for the dedication of Jovan, our daughter, or maybe for an Easter service, he would attend church with me.

One night he accompanied me to a Kenneth Hagin meeting at Crenshaw. I wasn't feeling well and had decided to go and be prayed for by Dr. Hagin. After the ministry of the Word and before the healing service, Dr. Hagin gave an altar call. James lifted his hand in obedience to the call of God.

The memory of that wonderful event is as vivid in my mind as if it had happened last week. I was ecstatic. He and several other respondents walked down to the front of the auditorium and were led away to a room for counseling. Three years after committing my life to the Lord, I saw my husband commit his life to the Lord, too.

19

HIS PERFECT TIMING

It seemed as if everything in my life was in place, except for that burning, unfulfilled desire to sing. I wanted to sing for the Lord! I wanted to sing for anyone who would listen, but I knew I couldn't sing secular music again. I was totally sold out. Sold out to God. Sold out to the gospel message.

I wanted to record the album I never had a chance to record in secular music. I was either with a group, or with a production, or in a play, or singing background for someone else, though I always secretly desired to sing on my own. Here, finally was an opportunity to sing my heart out. To sing the right music and in the right way, but no doors were opening. It was a very uncomfortable and frustrating time for me because I was singing in the choir, which was okay, but I knew there was so much more.

I can remember getting angry with Dr. Price. I don't really know why I got upset with him. It seems as if we always get angry with the pastor for whatever happens in our churches. I also got "teed off" at our music director. It was very frustrating to hear others singing leads and solos and not be given a chance to sing out front.

God was still working on me, however. He was still purging me; He was getting rid of the rebellion that was left over from my previous lifestyle. There were still some areas in my life that needed to be purged. I needed to learn submission, faithfulness, commitment, tithing, giving, prayer, and walking in love. I needed to learn to be obedient to the pastor, to show up on time at church, and to work as unto the Lord. I had to learn how to be faithful in little things, and most of all I had to learn how to be patient.

Those were things I was not aware of at the time, but, as I passed the test in those areas, I would say, "Now I see the wisdom in why God had me sit down." But I was still eager to sing. I could see myself singing to large crowds. I could see myself recording a CD. I even asked our children, Jovan and James II, to pray with me. "Pray for Mommy's record deal," I would say. "Pray for mommy's record deal. Pray that God will give mommy a record contract, a record deal."

At two and six years old, they would pray, "Father, we thank you for mommy's rekkadeal. What's a rekkadeal, mommy?"

I said, "A record deal is when you make a contract with a recording company to record an album, or a tape, or a CD, and people go out and buy it."

That is what we were believing God for while I was learning lessons of submission and giving, lessons of being committed to my local church, and lessons on how to apply God's Word to my life. I would show up early to work at Crenshaw, do my best work, and sometimes leave late. I wanted to work for God, to serve Him, and to serve Dr. Price. I never gave up on my dream to serve God as one of His psalmists.

I began once again to write songs. One of the songs I wrote was called, "Lifting Up the Name of Jesus," which is really my testimony set to music. It is about drugs, false religions, and all the different people I tried to follow who didn't have the answer. It is about the low self-esteem and the fear. It is about all the things I experienced before coming to the Lord.

We did it to a very rhythm-and-blues, contemporary beat. Some people questioned why I would sing a song with music that sounded so "worldly," but God gave me peace about it. I said, "Lord, you know; if this is not you, just let me know."

He said, to paraphrase the Scripture somewhat, *"My Word does not return void. But it accomplishes the things I send it to accomplish."* I took that to mean that as long as I was singing His Word it was okay.

At this time, I had begun to sing for weddings and other small gatherings. People began to hear about me, and I would sing for women's conventions at other ministries and also for the memorial services at my own church. On the days I was scheduled to sing at a memorial service I would carry my black dress and pearls to work and get dressed in the ladies' room just before the service. Then I would go over to the sanctuary and sing. After the memorial service, I would return to my office, feeling as if I was at least helping people. I was satisfied with this for a while.

Later, I became frustrated again and began to say to God, "You know, I really didn't plan on singing for dead people, okay? This is nice, but I hadn't really planned on this, you know?"

God began to minister to my heart that I was being used to minister to those who were left behind, to the loved ones and family members of those who had died. Then I counted singing at the services a privilege and an honor and never murmured or complained about it again. In fact, I looked forward to the times when I could be part of the memorial services.

I began to make a special effort to find songs befitting a "home-going" service, a funeral, or a memorial service. I began to learn songs that would be appropriate for weddings, as well. I began to learn songs that could be sung just before the ministry of the Word of God. The right song is so important. God began to place in my heart the idea that I needed to prepare songs that would fit every occasion.

Although I was mostly writing uptempo and rhythm-and-blues flavored songs with Christian lyrics, God was giving me sound tracks and showing me which songs to learn. He did this in order for me to be an effective minister of the gospel in the office of psalmist. So, this went on for a while. I was very comfortable that God was using me someplace, anyplace—in memorials, weddings, or whatever else He had for me.

Around this time, James and I went to see the Winans at the Universal Amphitheater. I just loved Vickie Winans, who opened for the Winans group. She is one of my favorite singers of all time. She only sang two songs, maybe three. I leaned over with tears in my eyes and said to my husband, "I can do that. I can do what Vickie's doing. I can do that. I wonder why God's not using me." What a whiner I had become!

I identified with her and that is what I wanted to do. Sing! Just like Vickie.

James comforted me in his own way on our way home from the concert, and life began again the next day—back to work and so on and so forth, with the memorials, etc. The routine and the intermittent frustration continued until one day about six years after I had gotten saved, I reached a breaking point.

I told the Lord, "God, if I never sing another song, if I never record another record, if I never travel, that'll be okay. I'm going to serve you, because you have done so much for me. I don't care anymore. Whatever you want me to do, that is what I am going to do. I'm grateful to be saved, I'm grateful to be married, I'm grateful that I'm in my right mind, and I'm grateful that I'm not on drugs anymore. So, Father, I thank you and whatever you want me to do, I will do. If that means not singing at all anymore, then that is okay, too." And I meant every word of it.

Apparently, that was the key to the whole question of my singing: Was I going to do it out of my own desire, or was I going to sing or not sing out of obedience, like everything else I did for the Lord? I had given up living my life my way when I got saved and delivered. Now I had to give up singing and submit to His will for my life. That act of submission is called "dying to self."

20

GIVING UP ON MY WAY

The tables began to turn. Almost immediately, God began to speak to my heart about leaving my job. I began to hear in my spirit, *"Quit your job. Go home and prepare for full-time ministry."*

I thought, "Wait a minute! We can't do this. We can't afford for me to quit my job. We need the money I'm making just to make ends meet."

James was working at Lockheed Martin and refereeing football and basketball after work for high school and Pop Warner games, and eventually he also took a job delivering pizzas. The money I earned working at Crenshaw was helping us pay bills and meet a tax obligation.

I said, "Lord, you know I can't quit my job here. We need the money."

In fact, finally, we were at a place in our lives where we could go to a moderately priced restaurant on the weekends and have dinner with our family and not fuss and argue on the way home because we had spent too much money on the meal. So, I was really confused. Quit my job? Quit my job?

God began to send people to speak words of encouragement into my life. He sent a fellow employee at Crenshaw who never had more than half a dozen words to say to me before, yet she gave me some tapes entitled *Settle*

Your Calling by Sarah Utterbach. I listened to them. The tapes confirmed something God had already placed on the inside of me—I was called, it was time to move, and I had to move *now*. Instead, out of fear, I was dragging my feet. I procrastinated for months. I was working every day for an anointed, powerful ministry, but without a sense of purpose. Something on the inside of me wasn't happy. I was not settled in my spirit. I had no peace.

I enjoyed my job. I loved my pastor and my church. I knew I needed to be obedient to what God was saying, but fear had come in. In fact, I was nearly paralyzed with fear. So God began to send people like the lady with the set of tapes. He sent other people to prophesy and speak to my heart about the call of God on my life and that it was time for me to make my move. God also began to send people into my life with money. Yes, money!

A couple we knew and loved, but hadn't been particularly close to, except to fellowship with them from time to time, sowed a seed of $2,500 into our lives! Another lady I not only didn't know but probably wouldn't recognize if I saw her today, gave me a $1,000 check and said, "God told me to give you this because He wants you to put out a tape."

People just began to give us money, a little here and a little there. We were so careful to be good stewards of the money God was entrusting us with that we were literally shaking. We knew it was God, and we didn't want to misappropriate or misuse any of God's money. After much prayer and discussion with James, it was clear what we had to do.

I said to James, "Let's record 'Lifting Up the Name of Jesus,'" which I had co-written with Steve Sloan. Also, we decided to record "Fear Not, My Child," which I had heard Bishop Carlton Pearson sing on TBN. That was the song that actually triggered my resignation from Crenshaw. As Bishop Pearson sang, shackles of fear dropped from my ankles and wrists, and the spirit of fear left my heart and mind. I was free. Free from fear and free to quit my job. This was the big turning point.

I had called every prayer group in America, I think, to make sure it was God telling me to quit. After hearing Bishop Pearson sing the anointed words of "Fear Not, My Child." I immediately knew what I needed to do. I no longer had the fear. Deliverance came as I sat two or three feet from the television set. So that song had to go on the album. More than fifteen years later, "Fear Not, My Child" still ministers to me.

Another song I absolutely adored was, "Can You Reach My Friend?" It is a beautiful song of intercession. The fourth song I felt strongly about was, "Wounded Soldier." So we stepped out in faith, took the money given to us, prayed over it, and began to call people we knew in the music business. What an exciting time this was for me!

Things had changed drastically in the music industry in the six to seven years I had been absent from it. I didn't know that you no longer needed musicians to back you up in recording sessions. You could go into the studio with one eighteen-year-old whiz kid and a computer and make all the music in the world. I didn't know that. Although we tried to play it off, James and I had been out of the music industry for so long, we had to relearn the business, both creatively and technically.

So we took these songs, which I had found to be effective as I ministered to small groups and services around the Los Angeles area, and we went into the studio. Jerry Williams, the young man who was helping me produce the tape, brought in a teenage genius with a ponytail named

John Bokowski to help hook up all the music. Then I went in and began to sing.

That first custom-made tape consisted of those four songs only, because that is all the money we had and all the faith we had. We didn't want to take the time to "believe in" the rest of the money. It was as though the anointing had lifted for that. So we took the finished masters and found a place in the San Fernando Valley that manufactured tapes. In about two weeks, they were ready to be picked up.

Immediately, we saw that God was moving. We took tapes to Beverly "Bam" Crawford's Bible study, where I had been singing on Monday nights for the past several months. The first night we sold out. We had so many dollar bills and five-dollar bills lying all over the kitchen table that night that I could not believe what God was doing. We were able in a very short period of time to pay back some of the people who wanted to be paid back. Others did not want money back, but said, "Just take the money we planted in your life and replant it into someone else's life."

So we took the finances as they came in and paid $2,500 back to the one couple that desired to be reimbursed. We planted seed into other ministries as we were led and as additional money began to come in. Then God began to open other doors. A friend of ours, John Wilkes, who is a gifted sound technician, took my tape to radio station KMAX in Los Angeles. Reginald Utley, a representative and KMAX on-air personality, called and asked if I could enhance a couple of the songs so they could be played on the air. So we did. We went back into the studio and enhanced the high end so that the songs would sound better coming through the airwaves. Everything was a step of faith. One step at a time, and at every step we glorified God because we knew He was doing it. We weren't promoting ourselves. We couldn't promote ourselves, for we knew promotion comes from God.

After KMAX played the songs, record stores began to call our home and say, "We need thirty cassettes. We need ten cassettes. We need five cassettes. We need fifty. We need ten." It was amazing!

All of a sudden I had become a delivery person, dropping off cassettes all over the Los Angeles area to different Christian bookstores and mom-and-pop record shops.

Eventually, a distributor called and said, "Lady, I don't know who you are, but my name is Bob Williams of W&W Wholesales. I understand you have a cassette that's being played on KMAX. We're getting so many calls for it, and I would like to distribute it for you. Also, we think we could be a blessing to you as you would only have to sell to us instead of the ten to twenty stores you now cover."

So we worked out all the business details, and I began to take armloads of tapes to W&W Wholesales once or twice a week instead of the many smaller drops I had been making. It was wonderful.

After a while, my four-song cassette tape was number one on his charts. I cannot tell you how good this made me feel. Then, one day, on my way to the Wednesday-morning Bible study, I walked into W&W Wholesales with tapes, running kind of late and a little distracted. There was a man there who was visiting from Word Records, which was based in Dallas, Texas. Bob introduced us: "Helen, this is James Bullard from Word Records. James Bullard, this is Helen Baylor, the lady I told you about who is outselling all of your artists."

It was kind of funny and a little embarrassing. Mr. Bullard gave me his business card, and I gave him mine. But I was late for Bible study and I couldn't stay, so I hurriedly said goodbye and ran out, brushing off the chance encounter. "Wow, I just met someone from Word Records," I said to myself. "Oh, well, I had better not get my hopes up about that right now. I can't get too distracted."

I went on to Bible study. I believe I led praise and worship, then sat down and received the Word. As I returned from Bible study, walking in the back door of my home, the phone was ringing. Guess who was on the phone? It was James Bullard from Word Records. Oh, it was awesome! In a nutshell, he said, "We're interested in you. When can we meet? When can we talk?"

A day or two later, I got a call from Sparrow Records, whose agent had gotten my number from a mutual friend. Other record companies called from the New York area and from Los Angeles. In a matter of two weeks, four record companies called our home looking to sign me to a recording contract. I hadn't sent out a single tape. I hadn't sent out one picture. I hadn't sent out one resume. I hadn't made one phone call. I hadn't gotten in anybody's face looking for a break. All I had done was to be diligent to the Word of God. We also had been good stewards over the money God had entrusted to us.

We considered all four companies, but it eventually came down to Sparrow or Word. Back and forth I went. Back and forth. I couldn't seem to decide. I didn't know what to think. Finally, we prayed, "Father, where would you have us be?"

I believe God showed us where He wanted us to be, so I had a final meeting with two Word representatives at the Sheraton Hotel near Universal Studios. We had a nice lunch, but I was shaking in my boots the whole time. Then the anointing fell on me.

I told them if I had to choose between signing with them and doing what I was doing (singing for women's retreats, Bible studies, women's conventions or wherever the doors were opening), I would choose to continue doing what I was doing then. Then I wanted to jump out of my skin and slap myself. I thought, "That is not what you're supposed to say!" It was the anointing talking. It was the unction of the Holy Ghost that had come upon me. It was like I wasn't doing the talking anymore, and later, I was so glad I had followed the leading of the Holy Spirit.

I believe I was letting them know, "Look, no matter who you are or who you think you are, God is still on the throne of my life." I wanted them to know I will never compromise my stand, my integrity, and the things in which I believe. If I have to make a choice, I will stick with what I am doing before I will compromise by signing with any record label.

Later, they told me that my statement of non-compromise was the deciding factor. Up to that point in the conversation and in the meeting, they hadn't decided whether they wanted to sign me or not. After those words came out of my mouth, they wanted to sign me, and I praised God that I had listened to the voice of His Holy Spirit. Under normal circumstances, one wouldn't say those things while negotiating a record contract.

Saying, "If I had the choice between singing the Word of God for fifty or 500 people in a church or a record contract, I would pick singing for the church before I would sign a record contract," didn't make sense at all. I am so grateful to serve a supernatural God, who knows what should be said and when it should be said. That comment changed the whole outcome of the meeting. Over the next three or four months, we worked out the details. I still sang. I still did meetings. In fact, the deal took so long that I had some questions as to whether or not I was really going to sign with Word at all. It seemed as if all of the details we were hammering out were taking forever.

I had run into a couple of attorneys who were going to help me get a good deal, attorneys who weren't very good with entertainment law. I had run into people who wanted to represent me managerially, who didn't have the right motives. So all these areas had to be dealt with between the time I first met with James Bullard and when I actually signed. Miraculously, I was introduced to Phalen G. (Chuck) Hurewitz, an outstanding entertainment attorney, who helped us get the best record contract possible. Even after all these years, we still enjoy a friendship and a business relationship.

I don't know how I stood the tension, except by understanding that the enemy was trying to rob me and God was trying to bless me. I had to walk by faith. By not doing anything personally to get the contract, not doing anything to get an audience with the record label, I knew that God was in it. If it worked, He had to do it. It worked; therefore, God was in it.

When we signed, there was enough money after paying tithes and so forth to pay down on our first home, which was located in Perris, about seventy miles east of Los Angeles, far away from all of the gang activity and drive-by shootings—but also seventy miles from our home church, Crenshaw Christian Center.

21

A Brand-New Chapter

This was a brand-new chapter in my life. God was turning the pages, as it were, and it felt good. We were so excited. Our children could play in the front yard of our new home without fear, and we planted orange and lemon trees in the back yard and put in a patio so we could entertain. It was so wonderful in spite of the much longer commuting times involved.

We ended up driving back and forth to the studio in Los Angeles when I made my record. James was driving back and forth to Lockheed in Burbank, which was even farther. He was spending two and a half hours on the freeway one way, but we were willing to make the sacrifice so our family would have a safer environment. The commute was a joy, knowing that we finally owned our own home.

We were so excited about what God was doing in our lives. It pays not to be weary in well doing and not to faint. The Word of God says that we will reap in due season if we faint not. We were beginning to see the payoff for diligence, hard work, standing on the Word, and not giving up.

Our new home was a simple, little three-bedroom, two-and-a-half-bath house, but we loved it. We were driving more and enjoying it less, yet we were being obedient to God. We would get up at 5:00 or 5:30 on Sunday mornings to get ready for church, driving sometimes in the rain. By then I was doing special music in rotation at Crenshaw as a soloist. I was still involved as a volunteer in the helps ministry, still tithing, still giving, still a wife, still a mother. God was blessing us and proving that He who promised is faithful. He truly does give us the desires of our hearts.

Now that I had signed with Word, we needed a producer to make my first album. So we called around, but either people were too busy or we didn't have a large enough budget for them, or whatever the case was. Then the bright idea came to go back to the young man, the genius with the ponytail, John Bokowski, who laid the tracks for our first tape.

We took those first four songs from the tape and re-mixed them, then did six additional songs. My first album was issued by Word in 1989. It is called "Highly Recommended" and is one of my best-selling albums. It is amazing that those songs still live and still minister. Everywhere we go, people comment on how they were blessed by that album. It broke records at Word for albums sold by a new artist.

My second album, "Look a Little Closer," also has done well. Then we did "Start All Over," which I recorded when I was pregnant with our last baby, Jonathan, who was born in 1993.

Jonathan responded to the music in a wonderful way. He could sing harmonies before he was two years old. He has extraordinary rhythm. He enjoys mimicking singers and we crack up laughing at him. All of our children are musically gifted. James sings and plays saxophone, drums and bass. Jovan sings and plays piano. She is also one of my background singers. Jeffrey plays keyboards and Jonathan is an aspiring drummer.

God began to open doors for me to minister all across the country through that first album. The first year I toured as a Christian singer, 1990-1991, took me to Africa with other musicians from my record company and other labels. God began to expand the ministry. From singing two or three songs, I was now doing full-fledged concerts—nine or ten songs with tracks.

For someone who had been a professional on stage most of my life, I found within myself a great timidity. Now, I was singing for God and not able to project confidence or control. I have heard ministers say that, if you are really sincere about serving God, there is a great awe that comes over you concerning the responsibility of handling His Word.

Sometimes I wouldn't even want to say "praise the Lord" or "thank you" or "good evening" or "hello" or anything. I was so shy, so timid. Then God began to show me that it wasn't me doing the talking, it was His Spirit within me. It wasn't about me. I was just a yielded vessel. So I began to have the courage to share a little bit more, and I began to loosen up.

As God continued to heal my low self-esteem and as I learned how to feel good about myself, He began to show me that the Body of Christ truly loved me and loved my music. He showed me that the adulation in the secular world isn't really love, but a fickle applause that can turn on you without warning. So I began to feel more and more confident about myself and more and more comfortable about ministering in front of people. I began to share bits and pieces of my testimony—not for sensationalism, but because of the unction of the Holy Spirit.

Also, I would find that each time I shared my life story with the audience that people were there who needed to hear what I had to say. Most of the time someone would have the faith to receive Jesus as Savior and Lord.

Like most young ministers, after a concert, I would second-guess or ask other people or my husband how they thought it went. Or I would wonder why I had said certain things. I would say, "Wow, I had no idea I was going to say that!"

I would ask James, "Do you think I should have told them that? Do you think that was too much to tell?" In so doing, I would torment myself.

God was dealing with some of the hurt and pain of my past. But I wish He hadn't dealt with me in front of everybody! However, He is God and He knows best, and that is the way He chose to deal with me. As I began to share more and more of my testimony, I became less and less an entertainer and more and more of a minister. It got to the point that I almost despised the spirit of entertainment, even though that was my background, and entertainment sometimes is a part of what we do as Christian artists. There has to be an element of entertainment; otherwise, people will go to sleep. You have to keep people's attention, but you do that by the anointing and by submitting your gifts and talents to the Holy Spirit.

It began to really bother me anytime I felt I was being pulled on to entertain, however. I began to bind that spirit in my concerts, and then I started to see people get saved. At first, I would do my concert in a church and then turn the service over to the pastor to give the altar call. I would see people come down front and get saved. The Holy Spirit would tell me, *"You can do that. You can give your own altar call, you know."*

I would say, "Yeah, I know, but I would rather the pastor do it. He has the anointing to do that," and I would argue with the Holy Spirit.

The Holy Spirit would answer, *"No, next time you give the altar call."*

I will never forget the first time I obeyed and gave an altar call—about three people showed up, and I was so embarrassed. I felt as if the altar should have been full.

However, God said, *"No, there is rejoicing in heaven over one that gets saved."*

God never, never treated me harshly. The Holy Spirit was never hard on me. He would simply teach me. Also, I tried to observe other people and how they gave altar calls, but God said, "Get your eyes off man. Do it by My Spirit, but be yourself. Give it the way you feel it, Helen."

So I quit saying, "Every head bowed," and began to say, "If you need to get saved, now is the time. If you want to receive Jesus, come down front."

The altars at my concerts began to be filled with people. As I started to share more and more of my testimony, the altars would fill up more and more. Sometimes people would begin to come down front before the altar call was given, perhaps on a particular song, like "Can You Reach My Friend?" or "Hunger for Holiness."

I began to see God's hand in my life, and then it came home to me what grandma meant when she said, "God's gonna use you one day." I saw God using me to bring about a change in people's lives. This happened—not because of me, or anything I had done or not done—but because I yielded myself to Him and was obedient to flow with His Spirit.

As I began to share more and more of my testimony, I eventually got to the point where I could give nearly all of it. (I probably will never give it all, because that would take too long.) However, I began to share about the drugs and some of the things I went through before I was delivered. In 1994, God, by His Spirit set me up for a wonderful blessing. He opened the door for me to do a benefit concert at Crenshaw Christian Center, my home church at the time. The only money we received was enough to pay the musicians to perform with me. Other than that, James and I donated our time to benefit the church's elementary, junior high, and high schools.

I was nervous, because I was in my home church, where I especially wanted to do an excellent job. It was nerve-racking. With the help of one of my record producers and drummer, Bill Maxwell, I was surrounded by some of the world's finest musicians. You couldn't have picked a better band than I had that night—eight musicians and three singers. We also had some of the best lighting and sound technicians in the industry.

We prayed; we loved God and worshiped and praised Him in our dressing rooms before we went on stage. The only thing I said to the band was, "I will probably give my testimony right before we do 'Lifting Up the Name of Jesus.'" Then we went out and did the best job we could do. That night, God put it all together. My testimony came out sounding as though we had composed a song of it. It sounded like we had rehearsed it. It was awesome.

As I began to share my life, the keyboard player, Greg Mathieson, began to play these beautiful chords beneath me. The anointing fell in Crenshaw's FaithDome as I shared and sang some of my testimony as the unction came upon me to do so. Then I would talk some more. A beautiful melody and inspired words came out of my spirit. Now, everywhere I go people ask, "Are you going to sing, "Praying Grandmother"? That is what they call the testimony I gave during that concert. We entitled the testimony song, "Helen's Testimony," but many people still call it, "Praying Grandmother."

Greg told me later, "Helen, I've never played beneath a message before. I've never played while someone was speaking or preaching before."

As we were editing the video, one of the camera shots caught his fingers, and they were literally trembling as he played, the anointing was so strong on him. The reverence and the fear of God was so strong on both of us, as well as the other musicians, that it seemed as though we had rehearsed this testimony, but we hadn't. After the concert, we had wonderful fellowship. Pastor Price came backstage, met the band, and thanked everyone. The church graciously gave us the footage in return for doing the concert. So we took the tape home and kind of "sat on it" for a while.

Then we thought, "Why should we sit on this?"

James and I had never edited a video before, but God began to show us how to edit. Editing requires watching all the different camera angles on several different screens and choosing the best of them all. Then all of the chosen shots must be put together to look as natural as if you were in the audience.

It was just James and myself most of the time, along with Chris Gregory, an editor we hired to help us. Then Bill Maxwell, who has years of experience in television, came in toward the end of the job, and he was absolutely a lifesaver. He helped us pick some of the better shots and put them into the right sequence and made sure the audio lined up with the video. Bill was brilliant. Editing is a very tedious process, but I enjoyed it.

God blessed us to executive-produce the video as well as the album we made from that concert. There are a lot of things that have to be done to make a video or album professionally fit for airplay and for consumers to buy. By His Spirit, God anointed us to do it. We called it *The Live Experience*.

When we released the album from this benefit performance, it jumped onto the gospel and Christian charts. It stayed at number one on the gospel charts for about thirty weeks, I believe. It was on the charts for more than a year and in the top ten for months.

So God knew exactly what He was doing. We began to get calls from women's and men's prisons. We got phone calls from people all over the world, people who were hurting—young people, old people, black and white, Baptist and charismatic. God was moving by His Spirit on this album with the testimony about my grandmother's prayers. It was proof to me that my testimony is what God had wanted to use all along.

The music, the albums, the recordings, and the songs, yes, that was great, but He wanted me to get my story out. He wanted me to be able to tell that I once was lost, but now I am found. He wanted me to be able to tell that Jesus is still alive and on the throne. Doors have opened for me to do so many things that were not possible before *The Live Experience*. It all came about by being obedient to God's Word and by being willing to give.

Since the release of *The Live Experience*, I've done five other projects: *Love Brought Me Back, Greatest Hits, Helen Baylor Live...My Everything* and *Full Circle*, for MCG Records, and guess what? James Bullard, formerly of Word Records, is the founder of MCG. Isn't it awesome how God brings us *full circle*?

My husband, James, and I are also teaching now, and we are doing seminars, sharing with God's people who desire to be used in music ministry, or in the area of helps.

We have several things we impart to people to better prepare them to serve God. We explain to them the importance of God's Word, and we take them through several steps: integrity, excellence, preparation of the heart, guarding the anointing, etc. However, we don't teach a how-to session on getting a record contract, because we know not everyone will get a record contract.

I can't imagine what would have become of the little girl from Oceanside if it had not been for the love of Jesus and if my grandmother had not prayed and "stood in the gap" for me, and all of her "grands," as she used to call her grandchildren. Neither can I imagine how I could continue to live the victorious Christian life without the infilling of the Holy Spirit, and the practical application of the Word of God in my life on a daily basis.

The Christian life is not without struggles and pain, but with Jesus on my side, I've been able to conquer everything, including low self-esteem, sickness, drug addiction, debt, and marital woes. Jesus always causes me to triumph, and I am assured that I will never be left alone or forsaken, and that nothing can ever separate me from the love of Christ.

We just thank God for our salvation, for our deliverance, and that the call of God is on our lives. Most importantly, we thank God for the fact that we are obedient to His Word and are willing to step out by faith to do what He asks us to do. In future writings I intend, with the help of God, to share the many victories I've experienced in my journey.

I am glad that God does not take back the things He gives us like the devil does. The devil gave us everything we desired, and then he snatched it back and turned us into drug addicts. But today we can boldly say that Satan is defeated in our lives.

118

However, if all of it went away tomorrow—all of the excitement, all of the houses and the lands, all of the fame and the fortune—James and I would still serve God with the same fervor we now have. God is taking us from glory to glory to glory to be a witness to His people and to the world that Jesus, the Christ, is alive and well and is awesomely powerful. We will forever praise His name.

22

In Conclusion

In the years since I began my journey with Jesus, I've learned more than the pages of any book can hold. I'm learning new things constantly, about myself, about my world, about the Word, about God's promises to me, about others, and the list goes on.

I'm also discovering the potential for greatness that every believer possesses. In my quest over the years to be the best that I can be, I've come to the conclusion that without Christ I am nothing (John 15:5), but with Him I can do all things (Philippians 4:13).

It may be a cliché to some, but the truth is, only what we do for Christ will last. As I've abounded with material blessings, from poverty and lack to houses, cars, clothes, and jewelry, I've had my share of trials and tests. And, as you probably know by now, I have come out on top every time.

I wake up every day to the new mercies of the Lord, ready to dominate every negative circumstance and able to bring every thought into subjection to the Word of God. On days when depression and heaviness try to lord themselves over me, I'm able to proclaim instantly that this is the day that the Lord has made. I will rejoice and be glad in it. I have found out that I cannot stay depressed or in a negative frame of mind too long. I just remember where I was before God delivered me, and where I am now. I may begin to shout or do a little dance when I reflect on God's goodness and faithfulness in my life.

The love of God is so vast, so powerful and so compassionate it's impossible to fully understand. How could a person with a limited education, a troubled upbringing, and a tragic young adulthood, end up being known worldwide, except by the love and grace of God?

Before the foundations of the world, God knew you and me. He knew what we would have to face. He knew every road we would travel. God saw our tears and felt our heartbreak. He saw us coming out on top—victorious! His love is so great that He gave His only Son (Jesus) that whosoever (that's me and you) would believe in Him would not perish but have everlasting life! Thank God for Jesus.

The Word also teaches us that Jesus came into the world that we might have life and have it more abundantly. It is so incredible to me that God would give His Son for us and that His Son would give His life for mankind. What a great love!

As you're reading this, I am enjoying the call on my life that sends me around the world singing, testifying, and teaching the Word of God. I am continuing to reach for God's best, as our ministry prayerfully conducts music and art seminars across the country. The years spent in the music industry, secular as well as Christian, have given me a wealth of knowledge, which I plan to use to produce and distribute Christian music all over the world.

There is so much left to do. I feel as if I am only at the halfway mark. I am looking forward to the next several years. As the Lord leads, I know the next season of my life will be filled with successes and triumphs because of His great love. I've finally found the love I'd been searching for all my life—in Jesus.

There truly is no greater love.

Prayer of Salvation

Dear God in heaven,

I want to know the same miracle-working God that Helen Baylor knows. I believe you are the God of love and deliverance. I confess Jesus as my Lord, and I believe in my heart that you raised Him from the dead. I receive Jesus right now as my Savior and Lord. According to the Bible, I am now saved. Thank you, heavenly Father.

Let me be the first to congratulate you for praying the above prayer. You are now a child of God, and you have all the rights—including healing, prosperity, safety, and the list goes on—that are due any other child of God. Now, I pray that you are led to a good Spirit-filled, Bible-believing, Bible-teaching ministry, and learn how to operate in those rights.

God bless you.

HELEN BAYLOR

DISCOGRAPHY

1990	*Highly Recommended*	(Word Records)
1991	*Look a Little Closer*	(Word Records)
1993	*Start All Over*	(Word Records)
1995	*The Live Experience*	(Word Records)
1996	*Love Brought Me Back*	(Sony)
1999	*Greatest Hits*	(Word Records)
	Helen Baylor ... Live	(Verity)
2000	*Super Hits*	(Sony)
2002	*My Everything*	(Diadem Music)
2006	*Full Circle*	(MCG Records)

VIDEOS

1995	*The Live Experience*	(Sony)
1999	*Helen Baylor ... Live*	(Verity)

AWARDS

1991   6th Annual Stellar Award for Best Female Contemporary Performance

1993   8th Annual Stellar Award for Best Female Contemporary Solo Performance

1994   25th Annual Dove Award for Contemporary Gospel Album, *Start All Over*
25th Annual Dove Award for Contemporary Gospel Recorded Song, *Sold Out*
9th Annual Stellar Award for Best Female Contemporary Album

1995   1st Annual Soul Train Lady of Soul Award for Best Gospel Album, *The Live Experience*

1998   13th Annual Stellar Award for Best Female Contemporary Performance

APPEARS ON:

1991	Babbie Mason, *Standing in the Gap*
1993	David T. Clydesdale, *One Special Christmas*
	Gospel Pie in the Sky
	Operation Angel Wings
1994	*Sisters: Songs of Friendship, Joy and Encouragement for Women*
1995	Justo Almario, *Count Me In*
1996	*Unforgettable Duets, Vol. 1*
1998	Phil Driscoll, *Live With Friends*
	Real Meaning of Christmas, Vol. 2
	Touched by an Angel: The Album
	WoW Gospel (1998-2001)
1999	*Real Meaning of Christmas, Vol. 3*
2000	*Verity Presents the Gospel Greats Live, Vol. 4: Women of Gospel*
2001	*Songs for the Soul, Vol. 1*
2003	*God's Leading Ladies* (EMI)

Helen Baylor's anointed music can be found wherever tapes and CDs are sold.

PHOTOS

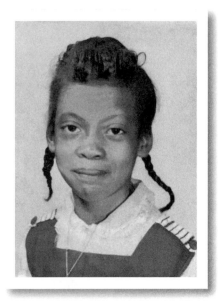

Me at 6 years old.

At 14 years old, I get a hug
from blues legend B.B. King.

Helen Baylor

The Soulettes, from left to right,
Cheryl Alexander, my sister Diane Lowe, Saundra
"Pan" Alexander, and Ruth Ann Scott (deceased).

On stage in one of the
many productions of *Hair*.

Me with the Captain & Tennille (1976).

Me and other members of
R&B group Side Effect (1976).

Helen Baylor

A duet with Chaka Khan.

My maternal grandmother, Minnie Hudson,
and mother, Melva Lowe.

Paternal grandmother:
Me with Mama Frances Lowe

Four generations: From the oldest to the
youngest—Grandmother Minnie Hudson holds
my daughter, Jovan, as Melva and I look on.

My friends, gospel artist Phil Driscoll, left,
and producer, Bill Maxwell (1993).

My two distinguished Dove Awards (1994).

Crenshaw Christian Center pastor, Dr. Frederick K.C. Price,
offers a hug after my ordination (1993).

Me and Side Effect members reunite during *The Live
Experience* recording at Crenshaw Christian Center (1994).

The 700 Club's Ben Kinchlow with me and JB.

Guitarist Paul Jackson, Jr., left, with me
and musician-writer Marciael Homes (deceased).

In the studio with the legendary
pianist Joe Sample (1993).

In the studio with famed blues
and R&B singer Mable John.

My dad, Ennis, and mom, Melba Lowe.

Me and Chaka Khan.

In the studio with "fifth Beatle," Grammy
winner Billy Preston (1996) (deceased).